A Taste of HAWAII

A Taste of HAWAII

New Cooking from the Crossroads of the Pacific

Jean-Marie Josselin

Photographs by Martin Jacobs

Illustrations by Coco Masuda

STEWART, TABORI & CHANG

NEW YORK

Prop styling by Linda Johnson
Food styling by Deborah Mintcheff
Edited by Ann ffolliott

First hardcover edition published in 1992 by
Stewart, Tabori & Chang
A division of U.S. Media Holdings, Inc.
115 West 18th Street
New York, NY 10011

Distributed in Canada by
General Publishing Company Ltd.
30 Lesmill Road
Don Mills, Ontario, Canada M3B 2T6

The Library of Congress has cataloged the original edition as follows:

Josselin, Jean-Marie.
A taste of Hawaii: new cooking from the crossroads of the Pacific/
Jean-Marie Josselin; photographs by Martin Jacobs.
p.   cm.
Includes index.
Hardcover ISBN 1-55670-191-8
Paperback ISBN 1-55670-993-5
I. Cookery, Hawaiian. 1. Title.
TX724.5.H3J67 1992   91-37797
641.59969—dc20   CIP

Printed in Japan

10 9 8 7 6 5 4 3 2 1

This book is dedicated
to the memory of my grandmother,
Rose Emonot.

Contents

ention Hawaii and everybody has a different idea. Silky black sand beaches and sensuous surf, if they've seen the travel ads. Natives wading out to boats to greet the tourists, if they've seen too many old movies. Glamorous, sinister images of Waikiki, if they've watched a lot of television.

Mention Hawaiian food and people also have funny ideas. Pineapple. Cubes of things in a pineapple. Drinks. Little decorative umbrellas in drinks. Luaus, with a pig roasting on a spit over a beach fire. Poi, lots of poi, whatever they think that is.

The truth is that Hawaii is a tropical state unlike any other in the United States. Our eight islands—Big Island (Hawaii), Maui, Oahu, Kauai, Molokai, Lanai, Niihau, and Kahoolawe— are 2,400 miles west of California in an otherwise unpopulated portion of the Pacific. These main islands, along with 132 smaller islands, reefs, and shoals, are scattered across 1,523 miles of the Pacific, southeast to northwest across the Tropic of Cancer.

There isn't much wading in the water to meet people these days, since most tourists arrive by airplane. Waikiki is densely built and urban, but a few miles away there is the wildlife preserve of Hanauma Bay beach.

Hawaii is that rare phenomenon of a truly multiethnic society, the most diverse in the United States and possibly the world. It all began with travelers from the South Pacific islands of Polynesia. During the last two centuries, since their discovery by Europeans, the Hawaiian islands have attracted explorers, merchants, investors, and workers from England, France, Russia, the United States, China, Japan, Korea, Samoa,

Africa, the Philippines, Puerto Rico, Spain, Portugal, and Southeast Asia.

The astonishing, high-energy confluence of East and West expresses itself in the everyday life of the Islands—in everything from language and religion to food and art. Even after thirty years of statehood and the development of tourism as the number one industry during the 1960s, Hawaii remains unique: a Hawaiian-Asian-American-Polynesian rainbow of life.

As for our food, it is based on an immense variety of fresh, natural ingredients, abundant in texture and taste. It consists of beautiful dishes, presented with flair and panache, which are extremely healthy because they are based on low-fat ingredients quickly and simply cooked.

What has really happened here—rather quietly and with no great coverage in the culinary press—is the evolution of a kind of world cooking based on the international array of ethnic cuisines on the Islands, the availability of fresh, high-quality ingredients, and the concern for a nutritious, low-fat diet. Add to this the Islands' style—lots of outdoor cooking, outdoor entertaining, a taste for informal elegance and beauty, and the importance given to family, friendship, and hospitality—and you have Hawaiian cooking.

There is pineapple, but it's not the dietary staple people imagine it to be. You're more likely to find it used in a sorbet or a salad with papaya, mango, banana, and kiwi than stuffed with cubes of meat. The luau—which some mainlanders think of as a "primitive feast"—has more the soul of a decorous, bounteous French family picnic, albeit with lots of family members and music on guitars. And poi, a very healthy starch rich in vitamins and derived from the taro, is still eaten, but very likely in combination with a Japanese-style vegetable dish, a Chinese stir-fry, or as an accompaniment to salty dried fish.

In the recipes I've gathered and created for *A Taste of Hawaii,* I offer the best of this spirited, contemporary Hawaiian cooking—the recipes with the most dash and distinction, the most taste, nutrition, and eye appeal—which characterize this trans-ethnic cuisine.

Readers who know a bit about Chinese and Japanese cuisines will find familiar ingredients and techniques, along with the challenge and fun of some new and surprising ones. Readers familiar with French and Mediterranean cooking will recognize some culinary landmarks—French chefs were a mainstay for many years at Hawaiian hotels and I, too, was trained in France—and lovers of spicy cooking will find happiness in the dishes inspired by émigrés from the provinces of China and Korea and the sailors and fishermen who came to Hawaii from Portugal.

I t is something of a miracle—resulting from two extraordinary navigational feats—that Hawaii was discovered in the first place. For millions of years these tropical volcanic islands were uninhabited by human beings.

A thousand years before Columbus's discovery of the New World, a band of Polynesians in search of land left their small islands in the South Pacific (probably the Marquesas or Tahiti). Navigating by the stars of the northern sky and praying to Laamaomao, god of the winds, they set sail with seeds and plants for the new land. These extraordinary navigators traveled in double-hulled sailing canoes carved from tree trunks with stone tools, lashed together with braided coconut fiber, and with joints caulked with breadfruit sap. Their sails were made of woven pandanus, boughs of the indigenous screw pine.

The Polynesian navigators based their route on the flight of the "Bird of the North." For many years they'd watched the migration of the Pacific Golden Plover—a small, graceful gold-speckled bird—with admiration. They reasoned that their eggs, which were never found on their islands, must be buried somewhere to the north.

After many weeks at sea, the navigators reached a paradise so rich it seemed conjured from their imaginations. They had discovered a majestic chain of islands, volcanic in origin, with wind-chiseled cliffs, deep valleys, and imposing mountain ranges. Here they found fantastic vegetation, a sea teeming with fish and seaweed, and interiors rich with trees and wildlife. They gave a name to one of the larger islands: Havaiki. They returned again and again, making the same miraculous voyage, eventually settling Havaiki and the other islands. Their civilization took root and flourished for more than a thousand years.

The land they found was fertile. They set about growing their native foods—taro, the nutritious, starchy root from which poi is made, coconuts, and bananas. They raised chickens and pigs. They cultivated special fish in man-made ponds—some saltwater, some fresh—for the exclusive use of the royal family. (A few ancient "royal ponds" survive.) Harvests were impressive and the new settlers thanked their gods with the traditional luau feast. The imu, an underground oven still used to bake the most succulent meats imaginable, originated among these Polynesian peoples. It is thought that the hula did, as well.

In 1776, Captain James Cook set sail from England on his third Pacific foray in search of the Northwest Passage linking the Atlantic and Pacific oceans. The great explorer planned to sail north of the Equator into the uncharted seas of the North Pacific for the first time. He traveled from England around the Cape of Good Hope to New Zealand, and onward to Tahiti. He reached an uncharted atoll north of Tahiti on December 24, 1777, and christened it Christmas Island. When he left the atoll he prepared for a voyage of more than 3,000 miles, setting a course for northern North America.

Sixteen days later, to the astonishment of captain and crew, a series of high islands rose from the waters. Landing on Hawaii, in Kealekekua Bay, Cook was filled with amazement at the existence of these islands and their inhabitants, who must—of necessity—have descended from superb sailors!

A speedy evolution into the modern age followed for the Polynesian people and their islands. British explorers were succeeded by British traders, then American, French, and Russian ones. Whalers arrived from Nantucket and New Bedford, Massachusetts. Missionaries came from New England—with the raw materials for New England-style houses, many of which survive, and a tradition of quilt-making, which took beautiful bright root in Hawaii.

Traders, merchants, and farmers from across the United States came to the islands of Hawaii. The holds of their ships carried great barrels of supplies such as grains, flour, and cereals—the starchy staples of Yankee diets for all-American cooking—puddings, pies, dumplings, gravies, and roasts.

During the early nineteenth century, the islands of Hawaii were planted with sugarcane, which had grown wild before the coming of the white man. This fateful economic step was to have a far-reaching political, sociological, and culinary impact. The massive planting of sugarcane and the conversion to the plantation system meant that many workers were needed, far more than the local labor supply could provide. Waves of immigrants came to Hawaii, and with each of these arrivals came a new culture, including new food, new ingredients, and new techniques that caused the modification of old habits and incorporation of native fish, fruit, grain, and meat. A series of culinary dramas in many acts began to unfold.

The Chinese and Japanese were the first to arrive. Rice—not bread—became the Islands' culinary staple. The Chinese brought their cooking spices and techniques (such as stir-frying) and complex Szechuan dishes. The Japanese introduced *shoyu* (soy sauce), sashimi, *bento* (boxed lunches consisting of rice, grilled fish, fried meat, and pickled plums), nutritious and infinitely mutable soybeans, succulent tempura, and satisfying soups of noodles and broth.

The Portuguese brought gutsy Mediterranean dishes with tomatoes, peppers, and hot spicy sausages; nutritious, economical bean soups; and fluffy, delicate *pao dolce* (sweet bread). Arriving Koreans unloaded their giant crocks of zesty kim chee and fired up barbecue pits for *pulgogi,* the traditional marinated

Chicken, Pork, and
Lobster Adobo

beef cooked over an open fire, and mouthwatering short ribs called *kalbi.* Filipinos brought their zesty adobo stews of fresh fish, meat, or chicken simmered in vinegar and garlic.

With the advent of jet transportation and the resulting development of tourism, French cuisine became part of the Islands' vocabulary. Classically trained French chefs maintained a determined—if somewhat lonely—vigil, cooking at the fancier hotels and restaurants. They prepared beautiful sauces and elegant desserts, integrating Hawaiian seafood into their menus in some cases, but often relying on air shipments of fresh or frozen Australian fish and never incorporating a hint of tropical produce.

In recent years, immigrants from Southeast Asia have come to Hawaii, bringing their subtle, beautifully spiced cuisine with its artful use of vegetables and seafood and fiery, aromatic curries, some of which trace their roots to India. Like the other cuisines before them, Thai and Vietnamese cookery have been welcomed by Hawaiians. If it is beautiful, interesting, healthful, and tastes good, they use it.

Because of the planting of sugarcane, and the immigration of foreign workers, Hawaii became an extraordinary patchwork quilt of people, each group using the bounty of Hawaii's tropical produce, singular seafood, and grain products in its own way. The newcomers found a variety beyond imagining, which must have been particularly welcome after months at sea, much of it spent in the darkness and squalor of a ship's hold.

Could they have found the food any more remarkable than I did? I was and am in wonder at what is here in Hawaii to work with: a bounty of fruit and vegetables, locally grown livestock, exotic grains, and a mouthwatering array of seafood, some of it indigenous to the Islands.

The Hawaiians were the best farmers of Polynesia and the tradition continues today. I buy produce from local vendors supplied by truck farms, or directly from the farmers of Kahuku, Waianae, UpCountry Maui, Waimea, and Kilauea, Kauai. Farmers in these regions grow the best onions, lettuce, watercress, papayas, and mangos. Some kind of fruit grows everywhere, from the thick of the jungle and the sides of roads to backyards and city parks.

Lilikoi (passion fruit) are small, smooth yellow wonders, sometimes growing wild on vines. Slice off the stem end, scoop out the luscious pulp with your tongue—a bit messy, but wonderful!—and you'll know why they're called passion fruit. More sedately, Hawaiian people use them to make wonderful fresh juices, pies, and flavorings for dessert.

Mangos grow wild all over the islands, on trees up to sixty feet tall. On the leeward sides of the islands, they ripen from May to July. On the windward sides, they last until October. Their delicate, apricot-colored flesh is indescribably delicious.

Guavas, abundant in the wild, are another small yellow fruit widely used in desserts and for juices as they're high in vitamin C. Their sweet fruit is also used to make jams, jellies, and preserves.

In Hawaii, bananas are not just the ubiquitous, bright yellow variety available at stateside supermarkets. We have more than seventy species—Hawaiians are connoisseurs of bananas much as Eskimos are of snow—with hundreds of variations. Some are used for peeling and eating, others for cooking.

Coconuts, one of the first plants brought to Hawaii by the Polynesians, are of legendary importance. When children were born, coconut trees were planted for them so they'd have fruit throughout their lives. You must live on a tropical island to experience all the different foods contained in one coconut. Drinking coconuts are large and green, each containing about a quart of water. Spoon-meat is a sort of natural custard inside the drinking nuts. Sprouted coconut meat is like a moist sponge cake. In addition to the coconut, the coconut palm supplies another delicious food. Heart of palm, also called "Millionaire's Salad," is found inside the trunk of a palm tree and tastes something like artichoke hearts.

We have hundreds of different kinds of avocados, which were brought from South America where they were originally cultivated by the Aztecs. Lychee nuts, with their thin red shells, are actually small fruits. When fresh they have a sweet, juicy white flesh; when dried, they assume their nutlike appearance. Our delectable macadamia nuts, native to Australia and first planted in Hawaii in 1892, now command a world market.

Hawaiian markets are filled with lush fresh pineapples,

Chinese Duck Soup

with Bok Choy

oranges, limes, kumquats, thimbleberries and blackberries, wild cherry tomatoes, tamarinds, and star fruits. All are of extremely high quality and have intense flavor, inspiring to eater and cook.

The islands are a paradise for fish lovers, what with delicious and distinctive mahi-mahi, a'u, ono, manini, ulua, and uku offshore. Hawaiian people eat about twice as much fish per capita as mainlanders; it's no wonder.

Mahi-mahi, or dolphinfish, has light, pure-tasting, and moist flesh. When first caught, mahi-mahi are blue and orange in color, but after a few minutes the skin turns a beautiful iridescent combination—blue, green, and gold.

A'u, an island delicacy, are broadbill swordfish or marlin. They are very hard to catch, with moist, white, delectable flesh. Ono, which means delicious in Hawaiian, are also called wahoo or king mackerel. They have white flaky flesh. Manini, eaten by many native Hawaiians, are small and caught with a net. They are very tasty and are widely available.

Ulua can weigh up to 100 pounds and have a dense, steaklike meat. Uku are moist, light firm fish—gray snapper—that grill perfectly. Ahi—yellowfin tuna—have distinctive pinkish meat and are prized for serving in sushi bars. Moi—the Hawaiian word for "king"—have large eyes and a sharklike head. They are impressive looking and tasting.

Other specialties include opihi, the small shellfish or limpets that cling to rocks, an island delicacy, eaten raw or grilled; aloalo, like tiny precious lobsters; crawfish, useful for spicy dishes and plentiful in the taro field streams; ahipalaka, gorgeous albacore tuna; octopus of various sizes, textures, and types; shark; and limu, the beautiful and nourishing island seaweed.

Hawaiian food is prepared in a dazzling array of ethnic approaches. Some were familiar to me before I came to Hawaii, particularly the Asian approaches such as the stir-fry methods of Cantonese cuisine, steaming, roasting, and the use of fresh ginger and other spices; Japanese broiling or grilling over charcoal; their seafood, seaweed, noodles, and rice. I knew the hot and spicy approach to Korean cooking, the use of sesame seeds and oils, and the lovely Korean salads.

But before I came to Hawaii, I certainly knew nothing of

the imu, the traditional oven dug into the ground. I had never tasted food prepared huli-huli, or roasted on a rustic outdoor spit over a fire made of guava and mango wood and banana and ti leaves. I had never experienced opah (moonfish), lehi (silver mouth snapper), or lomi salmon, prepared by massaging the fish with a marinade of chopped onions and tomatoes. I had never had fruit salads made with mango, papaya, and pineapple, passion fruit sherbet, or the Islands' Kona coffee.

Slowly, I began to penetrate the real Hawaii, to meet people, to eat in their houses. To have the honor and the fun of going to authentic luaus—an event something like a church supper, a New England cookout, a mardi gras celebration, and a fantastic fancy outdoor buffet (with the music of steel guitars) that goes on all day.

Initially, it was hard to get Hawaiian people to let me watch them cook. They were very modest about "their food," assuming I would want something "fancier," that I would want European food and not the local food. But Hawaiian food was delicious (I assured them), filled with fresh, zesty flavors and fruit and seafood, and prepared in a free-form, multiethnic way that dazzled me.

For one meal, I would see a Hawaiian cook mixing Japanese and Chinese vegetables with Asian and Polynesian spices, making a Portuguese-style bean soup or seafood stew using mahi-mahi and squid, and frying Puerto Rican–style banana fritters. I saw vegetables I had never seen before, including the all-important, highly nutritious taro, and I tasted tropical fruit of unsurpassed quality. I watched choreographic displays of artistic chopping and dexterous grilling, basting and baking, stir-frying, broiling, and other forms of rapid cooking that preserved taste, texture, nutrients, and color.

I began to go out with fishermen to see where they went for mahi-mahi, small clams, and the tiny black shrimp, found only in mountain pools. I began to gather kombu, nori, and other seaweed. I learned to use delicious Hawaiian tangerines and red snapper. I began to think about making tropical fruit sorbets.

I started to play around with ingredients, eliminating fatty cooking styles where possible, always using fresh local fish, and allowing myself to cross cultural divisions among several ethnic cooking styles as the Hawaiians—who are usually unaware of the origins of their ingredients and techniques—do.

When I studied cooking in France, I was taught that one must stick to the classical ingredients, recipes, and techniques to prepare a given dish. Use Polynesian grilling for a Chinese dish? Never! Use French techniques on Japanese vegetables? Never! Use Hawaiian ingredients in a French dessert? *Definitely* never. Still, I had an irrepressible desire to make guava sorbet, mango sorbet, and passion fruit sorbet—high in vitamins, low in fat, icy pastel delights.

One day, I shut myself in the kitchen and made a rice pilaf using Maui onions, macadamia nuts, almonds, and golden raisins. I threw in bits of chopped pineapple, mango, and lots of fresh ginger. Another day I made stir-fried wild mushrooms with bacon (so mainland American, but also Portuguese and Puerto Rican) with garlic and coriander. I made soup with Hawaii's tomatoes and tako (reef octopus) ceviche and wild watercress soup with Japanese pear and abalone. I continued with blue crab bisque, which I served with Filipino pepper crème fraîche and steamed salmon served with fresh coriander pesto into which I'd chopped some macadamia nuts. In an ultimate act of magnificent disobedience, I created a sumptuous pineapple-ginger crème brûlée, an elegant white chocolate–guava cake, and a macaroonlike chocolate macadamia cookie perfect to serve with tropical fruit sorbets.

Meanwhile, the contemporary style of Islands cooking was gathering force. Not with great fanfare—Hawaiians tend not to be self-promoting or evangelical about their cuisine. There was increased attention to the presentation of food, which was becoming more stylized and sophisticated. And to the continuing tradition of food as a way of solidifying ties of friendship and family—entertaining beautifully remains a part of everyday life. In Hawaii, people don't wait for an occasion to celebrate—they make one. Food becomes both the means and the end.

With my cooking, I try to frame—not overwhelm or disguise—an essential food or taste, to make a clear, distinctive, beautiful, and nutritious dish, one that conjures up what is special about Hawaii: the love of nature and the appreciation for basic quality, not artifice. Hawaiian cooking is getting the best basic ingredients and presenting them simply and honestly, not hidden in thick sauces and overwhelmed by needlessly esoteric preparations. There is something Asian about this idea, a way of showing respect for the food by presenting it honestly. And a way of showing respect for the person who is eating the food by presenting something close to its origin, healthful and fresh.

Cooking should be a pleasure for the cook as well as for the eater. It is much more fun—more satisfying and interesting— to cook with beautiful fresh food than to defrost cardboardlike fish fillets or to open a can. There is a deep pleasure in learning how to locate and select the best fish, poultry, and produce, a series of ongoing educational adventures that bring us closer to life itself.

These are the pleasures and adventures I hope to relate in this book. Cooking is like gardening. We all have a need to get our hands into the soil, even if it's a pot of herbs on the windowsill. We also have a need to cook, even if it's just learning how to grill a fish.

My approach to grilling fish is to learn something about the fish—(on this the French and Hawaiian parts of me are in perfect agreement!)—where it lives and grows, what it tastes like. Its shape, size, and texture indicate to students of cooking how to cook that fish and what seasonings and vegetables best accompany it.

Cooking is part of a process, an adventure. In this book, I want to convey the specialness of the Hawaiian cooking process. Learning the best greengrocers or farmstands (or supermarkets) for fruit and vegetables and herbs, learning about the life cycle and taste of different fish and shellfish, the color and texture of food—which comes only from washing it and cutting it on the cutting board—and creating the right menu for special occasions. Creating a menu that family and friends can help with, or a more formal menu that one creates in solo performance and presents for the captivation and nourishment (and bravos!) of guests.

I stress a devotion to finding beauty in everyday surroundings rather than fabricating something artificial. I would, for example, place a wild orchid on a serving platter of mahi-mahi, combining two local aspects of nature, but I wouldn't make an ice sculpture.

The willingness to live with, to combine and integrate a variety of cultures, is something distinctively Hawaiian that I loved from the beginning. Because this is a rainbow state of people with ancestors from many lands, the food I prepare is a synthesis of the healthiest, most appealing aspects of Asian, European, Polynesian, and mainland American cuisine—the most beautiful aspects, the most healthy, those with the most visual appeal and also the most potential for entertaining.

There is, again, something Asian about the "wholeness" of Hawaiian cooking: the idea of food and cooking as nourishment for the body, spirit, and mind. The idea that what pleases our senses is also good for us. That what we grow and prepare, we eat.

Though classically trained, I believe that one must move on from the standard repertoire of classic dishes. There are many more foods, techniques, and seasonings available to us than when the Western culinary archetypes were created. We have more cooking methods available to us because of technology, and more dietary and health requirements because of our greater understanding of nutrition.

My whole life changed when I found Hawaii—all for the better—and I would like to share the spirit and appearance of these beautiful islands with my readers.

1

Appetizers and
Salads

This dish is very tasty finger food. It was inspired by potato skins that I was served in an atmosphere-laden bar in New Jersey, which was my first encounter with American snack food.
• These potato shells can also be made with smoked salmon or other smoked fish. If you like Japanese food, try making them with unagi, or freshwater eel, prepared kayabaki style (grilled over charcoal) as in a sushi bar.

DEEP-FRIED RED POTATO SHELLS WITH SMOKED MARLIN

....

4 medium new red potatoes
1 small carrot
½ celery stalk
2 button mushrooms
8–10 snow peas
4 ounces smoked marlin
2 teaspoons peanut oil
1 teaspoon chopped garlic
2 teaspoons chopped fresh ginger
1½ cups oil, for deep-frying
¾ cup (3 ounces) shredded white
   cheddar cheese or mozzarella

Serves 4

....

· Cut each potato into 2 pieces and trim the bottoms so they can stand cut side up. Using a melon scoop, carve out the inside deep enough to hold the stuffing.
· Clean and cut the carrot, celery, mushrooms, and snow peas into small strips. Slice the marlin into strips the same size as the vegetables.
· In a small skillet or wok over medium heat, heat the peanut oil and stir-fry the garlic and ginger, stirring all the time. Add the vegetables and cook for 3 to 4 minutes, continuing to stir constantly. Add the fish and cook for 1 minute more. Remove mixture and set aside.
· In a deep-fryer, heat oil to 375°F and cook the potato shells for 3 minutes, until light brown and crispy. Drain on a paper towel.
· Preheat oven to 350°F. Stuff each potato shell with the vegetable and fish mixture and top with shredded cheese. Place right side up in a small roasting pan and bake for 3 to 5 minutes, until cheese melts.

- In a food processor fitted with a steel blade, combine the scallops, ginger, and lemon juice. Process on high for a few seconds at a time until the mixture is pureed. Add the cream, egg, salt and pepper, and cayenne pepper to taste, and process again until well mixed.
- Remove the mixture from the food processor and place it in a mixing bowl. Stir in 3 teaspoons of the tobiko.
- Dust a work surface throughly with cornstarch. Carefully wet each wonton wrapper with water along the edges, one at a time, and place 1½ tablespoons of the scallop mousse in the middle of each wrapper. Fold in half to form a semi-circle, and seal the edges by pressing with a fork.
- Poach the ravioli in boiling water for 1 minute. Remove with a slotted spoon, being sure to drain off all excess water. Place the cooked ravioli on a serving plate and garnish with the remaining tobiko, coriander, and sesame seeds. Serve with Lime-Ginger Sauce on the plate or as a dip.
- Note: If black sesame seeds are not available, use toasted white sesame seeds.

This dish combines foods from different ethnic cuisines. The flavors and textures are distinct. The tobiko (flying fish roe) is crunchy, which makes a nice contrast with the soft ravioli and the scallop mousse filling. The ravioli can be prepared well in advance and kept in the refrigerator. Be sure to dust them liberally with cornstarch so they don't stick to one another or to the dish.

SCALLOP AND TOBIKO RAVIOLI WITH LIME-GINGER SAUCE

. . . .

1½ cups medium scallops
2 teaspoons diced fresh ginger
Juice of 1 lemon
½ cup heavy cream
1 egg
Salt and freshly ground
    white pepper
Pinch of cayenne pepper
5 teaspoons tobiko (flying
    fish roe)
Cornstarch for dusting
12 round wonton wrappers
2 teaspoons chopped fresh
    coriander
2 teaspoons black sesame seeds
    (see Note)
Lime-Ginger Sauce (page 167)

Serves 4

. . . .

I'm very lucky because the waters around Kauai produce some of the best shellfish in the world. An experimental pound was started about twenty years ago, which can produce enough for the whole state of Hawaii. At my restaurant, the clams I serve have been out of the water for only a couple of hours. I always choose small clams, because they are more tender and juicy. • This sauce is flavored with green curry paste, which consists of green chilies, garlic, peppercorns, coriander seed, and cumin. These flavors bring out a whole new dimension in the clams. By decreasing or increasing the amount of green curry paste, you can control the heat of this dish.

STEAMED KAUAI CLAMS WITH LEMONGRASS AND GREEN CURRY SAUCE

· ·

1 cup dry white wine

2 teaspoons chopped garlic

1 stalk lemongrass, cut into
   small pieces (⅓ cup)

1 cup clam juice

4 dozen clams, in their shells

2 cups coconut milk

1½ teaspoons green curry paste
   (see Note)

¼ cup sliced basil leaves

½ teaspoon chopped fresh
   chili pepper

Serves 4

· ·

· In a large pan, combine the wine, garlic, lemongrass, clam juice, and clams. Bring to a boil, reduce the heat, and steam until the clams are open.

· Using a slotted spoon, remove the clams from the broth and set aside. Over high heat, reduce the liquid by one third. Then add the coconut milk and curry paste and mix well, cooking slowly for 2 to 3 minutes. Add the basil and chili pepper, stir, and remove from heat.

· To serve, place a dozen opened clams in a deep dish or soup plate for each person, then ladle the sauce on top.

· Note: Green curry paste is available in small cans in Asian stores, or you can make it following the recipe on page 216.

If you have a lot of time on your hands, you can cook your own crabs and pick the meat from them. But most of us don't have that kind of time, and processed crab meat from Maryland is a very good product. • Ponzu Dip can be purchased at Asian food stores, but it won't compare with the fresh citrus taste of this one. It can be made in advance and kept in the refrigerator for weeks. Leftover Ponzu Dip makes a wonderful marinade for chicken or shrimp cooked on the grill.

CRAB MEAT WONTON WITH PONZU DIP

- *Ponzu Dip*

  3 tablespoons light soy sauce

  2 tablespoons mirin (sweet
      rice wine)

  2 ½ tablespoons lime juice

  2 tablespoons orange juice

- *Wonton*

  Oil for deep-frying

  1 pound crab meat

  Pinch of cayenne pepper

  1 egg, lightly beaten

  1 tablespoon heavy cream

  ½ teaspoon chopped fresh
      coriander

  Juice of ½ lemon

  2 teaspoons diced red bell pepper

  12 square wonton wrappers

  Makes 12 wontons

· In a small bowl, combine the soy sauce, mirin, lime juice, and orange juice and set aside.

· In a deep-fat fryer, heat the oil to 375°F.

· In a mixing bowl, combine the crab meat, cayenne, egg, cream, coriander, lemon juice, and red pepper. Blend well.

· Place about 1 teaspoon of this filling in the center of each wonton wrapper. Secure the wrappers by bringing the corners together and pinching well, or simply fold the wrappers in half.

· Fry the wontons in the hot oil for 1 minute, or until they are golden and crisp. Serve at once with the dip.

- Prepare the grill.
- In a medium mixing bowl, soften the bean curd with the back of a spoon, adding the lemon juice and minced chili pepper. Set aside.
- Open each oyster and separate the meat from the muscle attaching it to the shell.
- On the hot grill, place the oysters shell side down and put a dollop of the bean curd mixture on top of each oyster. Grill for about 3 minutes, or until the bean curd has softened.
- Meanwhile, add the peanut oil to a skillet or wok and when hot add the garlic and cook until it becomes golden in color.
- When the oysters are done, remove from the grill, drizzle on the hot fried garlic, and top with the scallions.

This is a great dish for garlic lovers. When buying oysters, choose only those that are tightly closed and keep them refrigerated until just before they go on the grill. If you are not proficient in opening oysters, you can have them opened at the fish market. • Red bean curd is made from fermented soy beans and is used in many Chinese dishes to enhance and intensify the taste.

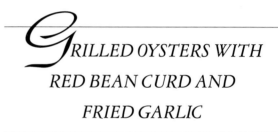

GRILLED OYSTERS WITH RED BEAN CURD AND FRIED GARLIC

. . . .

4 tablespoons red bean curd
Juice of 1 lemon
2 fresh red chili peppers, minced
2 dozen oysters, in their shells
2 tablespoons peanut oil
4 teaspoons finely chopped garlic
½ cup finely chopped scallions

Serves 4

. . . .

· Remove the hard muscles from the scallops and then season them to taste with the salt and pepper, ginger, and cayenne pepper. Set aside until ready to steam.

· In a bowl, combine the carrots, snow peas, scallions, and ginger, and set aside. Reserve the sesame seeds and basil sprigs.

· In a small bowl, combine the vinegar, salt and pepper to taste, ginger, and garlic for vinaigrette and mix well. Stir in the tangerine juice, then slowly incorporate the olive oil. Mix well.

· Using a large saucepan as the base, place the scallops in a steamer set over a small amount of boiling water. Cover the pan and let the scallops steam for 1 minute. Spoon the vegetables over the scallops and steam for another minute.

· To serve, arrange the scallops and vegetables on each of 4 dinner plates. Garnish each plate with a teaspoon of sesame seeds and a purple basil sprig and sprinkle with the Tangerine Vinaigrette.

Many recipes for scallops call for coating with flour and sautéing, which gives the scallops a nice golden color. But steaming them seals in all the juices and keeps the calories down without any loss of flavor. Don't add the vegetables until near the end of the cooking time, so they remain crunchy. If you like, you can serve these scallops on a bed of salad greens.

STEAMED SCALLOPS WITH TANGERINE VINAIGRETTE

. . . .

· *Scallops*
  20 large fresh sea scallops
  Salt and pepper
  Ground ginger
  Cayenne pepper
  ¾ cup julienned carrots
  ¾ cup julienned snow peas
  ¾ cup julienned scallions
  ¼ cup julienned fresh ginger
  4 teaspoons black sesame seeds
  4 sprigs purple basil

. . . .

· *Tangerine Vinaigrette*
  2 tablespoons white wine vinegar
  Salt and pepper
  1 teaspoon chopped fresh ginger
  ½ teaspoon minced garlic
  ¼ cup fresh tangerine juice
  ½ cup extra-virgin olive oil

  Serves 4

. . . .

Kim chee, the Korean national pickle, can be obtained with different heat levels at Korean markets. When making this recipe, prepare the salad first and deep-fry the squid at the last moment before serving.

SQUID SALAD WITH KIM CHEE AND BEAN SPROUTS

- *Salad*

  1 medium head green oak
     leaf lettuce

  1 medium head red oak
     leaf lettuce

  1 medium radicchio

  1 cup spicy kim chee

  1 cup fresh bean sprouts

  ½ cup shredded carrot

  ½ cup julienned red bell peppers

  ¼ cup Black Sesame Dressing
     (page 164)

  16 sprigs fresh coriander

- *Squid*

  Oil for deep-frying

  2 cups bread crumbs

  Salt and pepper

  1 pound squid, cut into rings

  1½ cups all-purpose flour

  5 eggs, beaten

  Serves 4

· In a mixing bowl, combine the lettuces, kim chee, sprouts, carrot, and red pepper with the dressing. Toss well and place in center of plate; garnish with coriander sprigs.

· Heat oil to 375°F. Season the bread crumbs with salt and pepper. Roll the squid rings in the flour; dip floured squid rings in the beaten egg, then in the bread crumbs, covering the squid well. Deep-fry until golden brown, about 2 minutes. Place the hot squid rings around salad, and serve immediately.

Green mussels, imported from New Zealand, are fun to cook with because they are large in size and beautiful in color. If they are not available, blue mussels can also be used. Always choose mussels that are tightly closed and clean, with no strong odor.
• You can prepare the sauce in advance and keep it warm in a thermos, or you can refrigerate it and warm it up before using.

STEAMED NEW ZEALAND GREEN MUSSELS WITH RED CURRY–COCONUT SAUCE

· Scrub and debeard mussels, place them in a steamer, and steam until they open, discarding any that remain closed. Place a dozen mussels in each serving dish, then top each mussel with a spoonful of sauce. Finish with a sprinkle of coriander and red pepper.

. . . .

4 dozen New Zealand green
   mussels, in their shells
1 cup Red Curry–Coconut Sauce
   (page 176)
Chopped fresh coriander,
   for garnish
1 red bell pepper, julienned,
   for garnish

Serves 4

. . . .

Nairagi, or striped marlin, average between 40 and 100 pounds
and are considered to be the best
marlin to eat because of their ten-
derness. Hawaiian sea salt, harvested in ponds on Kauai, has a
distinctive pink color because of
the deep red color of the earth
where the salt is harvested.

· In a medium mixing bowl, combine the salt, tahini, bay
leaf, thyme flowers, garlic, 2 teaspoons pepper, marjoram,
sage, and brown sugar, stirring well until ingredients are
well mixed.

· Arrange the seasonings on top of the nairagi and cover with
a piece of parchment or wax paper. Using a kitchen weight
or a heavy skillet, press down on the fish gently. Keeping the
weight on, refrigerate for 24 hours.

· When ready to serve the nairagi, remove the weight and the
parchment, and wash and dry the fish completely. Use paper
towels to absorb any excess moisture, and chill in the refrigerator for a couple of hours.

· In a small mixing bowl, combine the coriander, fennel, mustard, and sesame seeds, remaining ⅓ cup pepper, and basil.
Roll the reserved nairagi in the herb mixture, and refrigerate
until ready to grill.

· Prepare the grill. Grill nairagi for about 3 minutes on
each side. Serve immediately with Grilled Pineapple–Fresh
Coriander Relish.

GRILLED CURED NAIRAGI WITH SESAME TAHINI AND HAWAIIAN SALT

. . . .

1½ cups Hawaiian sea salt or
　coarse salt
½ cup tahini (sesame paste)
1 bay leaf
2 teaspoons fresh thyme flowers
2 teaspoons chopped garlic
⅓ cup plus 2 teaspoons cracked
　black peppercorns
1 teaspoon minced fresh
　marjoram
1 teaspoon minced fresh sage
1 cup light brown sugar
1 pound nairagi
½ cup coriander seeds
½ cup fennel seeds
⅓ cup yellow mustard seeds
½ cup toasted sesame seeds
½ cup chopped dried basil
1¼ cups Grilled Pineapple–
　Fresh Coriander Relish
　(page 168)

Serves 4

. . . .

When you are deep-frying the oysters, remember that you just want to seal the flavors, so they need to cook for only a few seconds.

CURRIED DEEP-FRIED PACIFIC OYSTERS WITH GARLIC-CHIVE SAUCE

. . . .

- *Garlic-Chive Sauce*
  ½ cup dry white wine
  ⅓ cup heavy cream
  1 cup (2 sticks) unsalted butter,
    cut into pieces
  1 tablespoon chopped
    garlic chives
  Salt and pepper

. . . .

- *Oysters*
  Oil for deep-frying
  1 cup cornmeal
  4 teaspoons yellow curry powder
  Dash of cayenne pepper
  24 medium oysters, in their shells

Serves 4

. . . .

· In a nonreactive saucepan over high heat, reduce the white wine by one half, add the cream, and reduce again by half. Over low heat incorporate the butter slowly, a piece at a time, stirring constantly, then add the chives. Season with salt and pepper to taste. Blend mixture in blender for 15 seconds, or until the chives are incorporated. Keep warm.

· Heat the oil in a deep saucepan to 375°F. Combine the cornmeal, curry powder, and cayenne pepper in a dish. Remove the oysters from their shells and reserve deep half of shell. Roll oysters in the cornmeal mixture until well coated, then deep-fry a few seconds until golden brown. Fill each reserved oyster shell with the sauce, then place the fried oysters back in the shells. Serve at once.

Ono is the Hawaiian word for "good to eat," which this fish undoubtedly is. The flesh of the ono is white and mild in flavor, and it doesn't have a lot of fat. If you can't get it, you can substitute mackerel. • If you like spicy food, this dish is for you. The mild fish, the pungent salsa, and the sour vinegar make for a strong flavor, great for summertime meals. If you don't like this much chili pepper, try substituting toasted sesame seeds.

PEPPERED ONO SALAD WITH PAPAYA AND CUCUMBER SALSA

. . . .

- *Salad*

  1 small head radicchio

  1 medium head baby
     romaine lettuce

  1 medium head baby
     Manoa lettuce

  8 arugula leaves

  ⅓ cup chopped cashews

  ⅓ cup shredded carrot

  ½ cup chopped shiitake
     mushrooms

. . . .

- *Fish*

  12 ounces ono fillet, cut into strips

  ⅓ cup olive oil

  Salt and cracked black pepper

  ¼ cup balsamic vinegar

  Juice of 1 lime

  2½ cups Papaya and Cucumber
     Salsa (page 174)

  Serves 4

. . . .

· Separate the lettuce leaves for the salad and run them under cold water to remove any dirt. Wash the arugula leaves. Dry the leaves in a salad spinner and then arrange them carefully on a large serving plate. Sprinkle the leaves with the cashews, shredded carrot, and shiitake mushrooms and set the plate aside.

· Brush the fish strips with some of the olive oil. Sprinkle with the salt and cracked black pepper.

· Heat a nonstick skillet to medium hot and add the remainder of the olive oil. Sauté the fish until it is medium inside, about 2 minutes. Remove the fish from the pan and drain on paper towels.

· Add the vinegar and lime juice to the skillet and deglaze the pan. Remove from the heat and set aside.

· Prepare the Papaya and Cucumber Salsa and set it aside.

· To assemble the salad, place the cooked fish strips on the arranged salad. Sprinkle the fish and salad with the sauce from the pan. Place the salsa on top of the fish and serve at once.

Here is a quick way to serve
something fresh and full of flavor.
The salad can be prepared in
advance and chilled. Kamaboko,
a processed fishcake, is found
in many Asian stores in the
refrigerated section.

· Fill a large saucepan with water and add a small amount of
salt. Bring to a boil and add the noodles. Cook until the
noodles are soft, about 2 minutes. Rinse in cold water and
drain well.

· In a mixing bowl, combine the noodles, ginger, cucumber,
scallions, crab meat, daikon, and carrot. Mix well.

· Combine the vinegar, sesame oil, peanut oil, soy sauce, and
sesame seeds in a small bowl and mix well.

· Place equal amounts of the kamaboko and nori in each of
4 serving bowls. Distribute the noodle salad among the
bowls, top each serving with 4 tablespoons of the dressing,
and mix well.

SOMEN NOODLE SALAD WITH CRAB MEAT

. . . .

• *Salad*

Salt

8 ounces fresh somen noodles
  (or dried noodles if fresh are
  not available)

½ cup shredded young ginger

1 cup thinly shredded cucumber

½ cup julienned scallions

1 cup crab meat

½ cup shredded daikon

½ cup shredded carrot

. . . .

• *Dressing*

⅔ cup rice wine vinegar

1 tablespoon roasted sesame oil

1 tablespoon peanut oil

4 teaspoons light or dark
  soy sauce

1 teaspoon black sesame seeds

1 teaspoon white sesame seeds

1 cup julienned kamaboko

¼ cup julienned nori

Serves 4

. . . .

*Soba noodles, made from buck-
wheat flour, are very delicate
but very flavorful. Cook them
for about one minute in boiling
water, rinse well under running
water, and drain carefully.*

SOBA NOODLE SALAD WITH SWEET SHRIMP ROLLS

- *Shrimp Rolls*

  Oil for deep-frying

  ½ teaspoon diced fresh
  chili pepper

  2 teaspoons chopped fresh
  coriander

  Juice of 1½ limes

  ½ teaspoon minced fresh ginger

  ½ teaspoon white sesame seeds

  12 large shrimp, shells removed
  but heads on

  12 wonton wrappers

- *Soba Noodles*

  2½ cups cooked, drained
  soba noodles

  ½ cup chopped red bell pepper

  4 tablespoons diced pickled
  ginger

  4 tablespoons chopped fresh
  coriander

  1 cup diced fresh tomato

  ½ cup bean sprouts

  ½ medium mango, peeled
  and diced

  ½ cup Black Sesame Dressing
  (page 164)

  Serves 4

· Heat oil to 375°F. Combine the chili pepper, coriander, lime juice, ginger, and sesame seeds in a bowl. Place shrimp in marinade and let sit for 15 minutes.

· Place a shrimp on each of the wonton wrappers, fold over, and secure shut by pinching the edges together. Deep-fry the shrimp rolls until golden and crispy, about 2 minutes. Set aside to drain on paper towels.

· Combine the ingredients for noodles and mix until well coated with the dressing. Serve the noodles alongside the shrimp rolls.

Okinawa spinach has a distinct, nutty flavor. When combined with shiitake mushrooms and pomelo sections, the result is very refreshing. If it is not available, use regular spinach, but it won't have the same texture or flavor. The pomelo is a citrus fruit, native to Malaysia, which may be an ancestor of the grapefruit.

OKINAWA SPINACH SALAD WITH SHIITAKE MUSHROOMS AND POMELO

. . . .

4 cups Okinawa spinach,
   loosely packed
4 cups pomelo segments
1 teaspoon grated fresh ginger
2 teaspoons diced chives
4 medium shiitake mushrooms,
   cut in julienne strips
Salt and pepper
¼ cup Black Sesame Dressing
   (page 164)

Serves 4

. . . .

· Remove the spinach stems from the leaves and rinse the leaves thoroughly in cold water. Dry them well. In a large bowl, combine the spinach with the pomelo, ginger, chives, mushrooms, and salt and pepper. Pour the dressing over the salad and toss until ingredients are well coated. Chill before serving.

This salad is particularly refreshing during long, hot summers. It is a perfect accompaniment to spring rolls.

GREEN PAPAYA SALAD

· Peel off the skin of the papaya and, using a grater, shred the pulp finely. Discard the seeds. Peel the cucumber and carrots, then grate them.

· In a mixing bowl, combine the papaya, cucumber, and carrots. Add the garlic, coriander, sugar, and lime juice. Season to taste with salt and pepper. Chill before serving.

. . . .

1 medium green papaya
1 large cucumber
2 medium carrots
1 teaspoon minced garlic
2 teaspoons chopped fresh
    coriander
1 teaspoon sugar
Juice of 2 limes
Salt and pepper

Serves 4

. . . .

Roasted duck, combined with the spiciness of kim chee and the sweetness of mango, makes one of my favorite salads. Many Chinese restaurants sell roasted ducks to take home, but if they are not available, see the recipe on page 215. The duck tastes best if it is kept at room temperature before using in the salad.

CHINESE DUCK SALAD WITH MANGO AND KIM CHEE

. . . .

1 tablespoon red wine vinegar

1 tablespoon toasted white
   sesame seeds

2 tablespoons extra-virgin olive oil

2 teaspoons roasted sesame oil

1 teaspoon hot pepper sauce

2 roasted Peking duck breasts,
   sliced

1 red bell pepper, cut into
   thin slices

1 small Maui onion, sliced thin

1 medium mango, with seed and
   peel removed

1 medium head radicchio

1 medium head Manoa lettuce

2 heads baby romaine lettuce

¼ cup chopped roasted peanuts

½ cup kim chee

¼ cup shredded carrot

3 teaspoons chopped fresh
   coriander

5 mint leaves, sliced thin

Serves 4–6

. . . .

· Combine the vinegar, sesame seeds, olive oil, sesame oil, and hot pepper sauce in a small mixing bowl, and set aside at room temperature.

· Cut the duck breasts, red bell pepper, onion, and mango into ½-inch pieces. Place in a large salad bowl.

· Tear the radicchio and the lettuces into bite-size pieces and add to the bowl. Add the peanuts, kim chee, and carrot, and toss. Pour the dressing over the salad, mixing well, and garnish with coriander and mint leaves. Chill before serving.

Poisson cru *means "raw fish"*
in French. In this dish, the crisp
polenta, the fish, and the spicy
wasabe and pickled ginger
make a fantastic combination
of textures and flavors. My good
friend Roy Yamaguchi cooked
this for my restaurant's first
anniversary celebration.

CRISP SHIITAKE POLENTA WITH POISSON CRU AND WASABE-SOY BEURRE BLANC

. . . .

- *Polenta*

  4 cups water

  Pinch of salt

  1 cup coarse yellow cornmeal

  2 teaspoons minced fresh ginger

  4 tablespoons (½ stick) unsalted
     butter, softened

  2 teaspoons peanut oil

  1 cup sliced shiitake mushrooms

  Oil for deep-frying

. . . .

- *Poisson Cru*

  ½ pound freshly filleted snapper,
     skin removed

  1 teaspoon minced fresh red or
     green chili pepper

  Juice of 4 limes

  Salt

  3 teaspoons chopped fresh parsley

  Wasabe-Soy Beurre Blanc
     (page 178)

  2 teaspoons finely julienned
     roasted nori

  4 teaspoons pickled ginger

Serves 6

. . . .

· In a large saucepan, combine the water and salt and bring to
  a boil. Slowly pour the cornmeal into the water, stirring constantly to avoid lumps. Reduce the heat, add the ginger, and
  continue cooking over low heat, stirring occasionally, until
  the polenta pulls away from the sides of the pan and the
  water evaporates, about 30 minutes. Mix in butter.

· In a small skillet, heat the oil and sauté the shiitake mushrooms. When they are cooked, add them to the polenta.

· Brush a baking sheet with oil and spread the cooked polenta
  onto the sheet, smoothing it with an oiled spatula. Cover the
  polenta with plastic wrap and refrigerate overnight.

· The next day, cut the polenta into the desired shapes. Heat
  oil for deep-frying to 375°F and deep-fry the pieces until
  golden and crisp. Drain on paper towels.

· Cut the fish fillet into thin slices and combine with the chili
  pepper, lime juice, salt, and parsley. Refrigerate for 1 hour.

· Prepare the wasabe-soy beurre blanc and set it aside in a
  thermos or a warm place.

· To assemble and serve the dish, place a piece of polenta on a
  plate. Place some marinated fish on top. Garnish with nori
  and pickled ginger. Pour some beurre blanc around the
  polenta and serve immediately.

· Note: When making this recipe, allow the polenta to become really stiff by letting it rest for a day in the refrigerator. If you don't want to deep-fry it, you can sauté or grill it
  until it is golden and crisp.

· Using a small knife, cut the root ends from the radicchio and separate each leaf without breaking. Remove the stems from the arugula and clean leaves under cold water. Clean and julienne all the remaining vegetables. Divide the radicchio among 4 plates, arranging each portion to form a large cup; add the arugula, dividing evenly among the plates.

· In a medium skillet, heat the olive oil and stir-fry the mushrooms, seasoning with salt and pepper. Add the lime juice, continue cooking for about 15 seconds, and then remove the mushrooms using a slotted spoon; set aside. In the same skillet, add the garlic and ginger and stir-fry the remaining vegetables. Divide the cooked vegetables among the 4 plates and arrange the mushrooms on top. Deglaze the pan with the balsamic vinegar and sprinkle over each portion.

This is a quick salad with a lot of flavors—very colorful and easy to prepare. The combination of balsamic vinegar with lime juice, ginger, and garlic is unusual and delicious.

STIR-FRIED SHIITAKE MUSHROOM SALAD WITH BALSAMIC VINEGAR

. . . .

4 heads radicchio

3 bunches arugula

1 medium carrot

16 snow peas

1 medium red bell pepper

5 teaspoons olive oil

8 shiitake mushrooms, in
   large julienne

Salt and pepper

Juice of 1 lime

1 teaspoon chopped garlic

2 teaspoons chopped fresh ginger

5 teaspoons balsamic vinegar

Serves 4

. . . .

This is my answer to tortilla chips and salsa. The scallops are spiced up and the combination makes for a wonderful contrast of flavors. But be careful—the ginger in the pesto is eaten raw and is therefore hot!

Wonton Chips and Charred Scallops with Hawaiian Pesto

. . . .

1 recipe Hawaiian Pesto
   (page 185)

. . . .

- *Wonton Chips*

   Vegetable oil for deep-frying
   4 round wonton wrappers,
      cut in quarters
   Salt

. . . .

- *Scallops*

   2 teaspoons paprika
   ½ teaspoon cayenne pepper
   1 teaspoon ground cumin
   Pinch of salt
   ¼ cup vegetable oil
   1 teaspoon roasted sesame oil
   12 medium sea scallops

   Fresh coriander sprigs, for garnish

   Serves 4

. . . .

· Prepare the Hawaiian Pesto and refrigerate until ready to use.
· Heat the oil for deep-frying to 375°F. Deep-fry the wonton quarters until crisp and golden, about 2 minutes. Drain well on a paper towel and season with salt.
· In a small bowl, combine the paprika, cayenne pepper, cumin, salt, and oils. Add the scallops, making sure that they are well coated with the mixture. Heat a skillet over high heat and sauté the scallops for about 2 minutes on each side.
· Place a scallop on a wonton chip and top with a dollop of Hawaiian Pesto. Serve on a large platter, garnished with sprigs of fresh coriander.
· Note: This recipe is also good with sliced ahi instead of scallops, but be sure not to overcook it.

Watercress is one of my favorite greens, and it is really fantastic when dressed with sesame oil.
• If you can't find kumquats, this salad is just as good when made with oranges.

SHREDDED POACHED CHICKEN SALAD WITH GINGER-KUMQUAT DRESSING

. . . .
- *Chicken Salad*

  1 bunch watercress

  1 cup bean sprouts

  ½ cup chopped red bell pepper

  3 Thai basil leaves, shredded

  ½ cup chopped jicama or water chestnuts, if available

  3 teaspoons chopped fresh coriander

  5 basil leaves, shredded

  2 cups shredded cold chicken
. . . .
- *Ginger-Kumquat Dressing*

  ½ teaspoon minced garlic

  ½ teaspoon minced fresh ginger

  8 kumquats, peeled and separated into segments

  2 tablespoons roasted sesame oil

  2 tablespoons light soy sauce

  Serves 4
. . . .

· Bring a large pan of salted water to a boil and blanch the watercress for about 1 minute, until bright green. Drain and immediately plunge into ice water.

· Drain the watercress thoroughly and combine with bean sprouts, bell pepper, Thai basil, jicama, coriander, and basil leaves. Add the chicken.

· In a small bowl, combine the garlic, ginger, kumquats, sesame oil, and soy sauce. Pour over the chicken salad and toss. Serve at once.

1 pound boneless and skinless
  chicken, cut into cubes
2 teaspoons red curry paste
  (page 216)
4 kaffir lime leaves, shredded
6 basil leaves, shredded
Salt
2 teaspoons minced garlic
2 teaspoons minced fresh ginger
½ cup rice wine vinegar
2 eggs
½ teaspoon minced hot green
  chili pepper
3 feet sausage casings
Rice Noodle Salad (recipe follows)

Serves 4

GRILLED THAI CHICKEN SAUSAGES WITH RICE NOODLE SALAD

- *Rice Noodle Salad*
  2 cups rice noodles, cooked
    and drained
  ¼ cup Green Apple Dressing
    (page 190)
  2 teaspoons minced fresh ginger
  ½ teaspoon minced garlic
  ½ teaspoon black sesame seeds
    or toasted white sesame seeds
  3 teaspoons chopped scallions
  1 teaspoon chopped fresh
    coriander
  ½ cup bean sprouts
  ¼ cup shredded carrot
  3 mint leaves, shredded

Makes 3½ cups

Sausages are fun to make. You can obtain the casings from your butcher. • Rice noodles, or rice sticks, cook rather fast and should not be overcooked or they will become mushy. Place the noodles in boiling water, stir gently, and cook for about half a minute. Drain them immediately and refresh in cold water

· Place the chicken in a food processor and pulse in on-off motions until the chicken is coarsely shredded. Transfer the chicken to a mixing bowl and add the curry paste, lime leaves, basil, and salt to taste. Mix well with a spatula. Add the garlic, ginger, vinegar, and eggs, and blend well. Add the chili pepper.

· Stuff the chicken mixture into the sausage casings, being careful not to pack them too tightly or else they will burst during cooking. Tie the sausages at 4-inch intervals. Let the sausages drain and then let them dry for 1½ hours in the refrigerator before grilling.

· Prepare grill. Grill sausages over medium heat for about 8 minutes, or until thoroughly cooked.

· Serve with Rice Noodle Salad.

· Note: Sausage casings, usually pork, come preserved in salt. You need to rinse them in running water for a couple of minutes to remove it.

- *Rice Noodle Salad*
· Combine all ingredients and refrigerate until ready to serve.

Gyosa are Japanese dumplings, which are fried until they turn a nice golden color and then steamed to complete the cooking. An easy dish, this spicy mix of Japanese and Thai cuisines can be prepared in advance, but it is best to cook the gyosa just before serving.

SPICY CHICKEN AND EGGPLANT GYOSA

- *Oriental Dip*

  ½ teaspoon red pepper flakes

  ¾ cup reduced-sodium soy sauce

  2 teaspoons minced pickled
    ginger

  ¼ cup julienned scallions

  2 teaspoons chopped fresh ginger

- *Gyosa*

  ⅔ cup diced chicken breast

  2 teaspoons red curry paste
    (see Note)

  3 teaspoons mirin (sweet
    rice wine)

  1 teaspoon minced lemongrass

  3 kaffir lime leaves

  4 basil leaves

  Salt

  2 eggs

  ⅓ cup eggplant puree (see recipe
    for Eggplant Caviar, page 150)

  Cornstarch for dusting

  12 gyosa or round wonton
    wrappers

  2 teaspoons peanut oil

  3 teaspoons water

Serves 4

· In a small bowl, combine the red pepper flakes, soy sauce, pickled ginger, scallions, and chopped ginger and set aside.

· In a blender, combine the chicken with the curry paste, mirin, lemongrass, lime leaves, basil leaves, salt, and eggs. Blend until mixture is the consistency of a mousse. Place mixture in a bowl and combine with eggplant puree; mix well.

· Dust a work surface thoroughly with cornstarch. In the center of each wrapper, place 1 full teaspoon of the mixture. Fold the wrapper in half, and use a fork to seal the edges tightly.

· Add the oil to a skillet and fry the gyosa for 1 minute, or until they are light brown in color, then add the water, cover, and steam over low heat for about 10 minutes, checking to be sure there is enough water to keep the gyosa from burning. Serve at once with the Oriental Dip.

· Note: Thai red curry paste can be found in Asian grocery stores in small cans. Once opened, it can be kept in the refrigerator for a month. Or you can make your own using the recipe on page 216. You can use more or less in this recipe, according to your taste.

· If you can find them, use gyosa wrappers, which are very white in color and will make a more attractive dumpling. But these dumplings will also taste good if you use wonton wrappers.

· Heat the peanut oil in a wok. Add the garlic and ginger, then stir-fry all the vegetables lightly so they retain their crunchiness. Add the soy sauce, oyster sauce, chicken, and chili pepper. Season to taste and let cool.

· Preheat oil in deep-fryer to 375°F.

· Place ½ cup of the vegetable mixture in each lumpia wrapper and roll, tucking in ends as you roll. Seal with egg yolk. Deep-fry lumpia until wrappers are crisp and golden, about 3 minutes. Serve with Curried Lime Dip.

Lumpia are the Philippine version of egg rolls and are very flaky. If you can't find lumpia wrappers, use egg roll wrappers.

DEEP-FRIED SMOKED CHICKEN LUMPIA WITH CURRIED LIME DIP

. . . .

Peanut oil for stir-frying and
   deep-frying
3 teaspoons chopped garlic
3 teaspoons chopped fresh ginger
1 medium carrot, cut into
   julienne strips
1 medium zucchini, cut into
   julienne strips
15 snow peas, cut into
   julienne strips
1 cup bean sprouts
¼ cup dark soy sauce
4 teaspoons oyster sauce
8 ounces smoked boneless
   chicken breast, diced
½ teaspoon chopped fresh red
   chili pepper
Salt and pepper
4 lumpia wrappers
2 egg yolks, lightly beaten
1¼ cups Curried Lime Dip
   (page 168)

Serves 4

. . . .

The lychee is native to South China. The harvest season is short, so retailers have a hard time keeping a good supply on hand. Check an Asian grocery for availability. If fresh lychees are not available, substitute canned.

· Combine the marinade ingredients. Place the chicken in mixture and marinate, refrigerated, for at least 2 hours. Drain the chicken and reserve.

· Prepare the grill. Brush on the peanut oil and grill the chicken until golden on both sides, about 3 minutes per side. Remove from grill and set aside. When cool, cut into strips.

· Preheat a wok over high heat. Add peanut oil and stir-fry the ginger and garlic until they release their fragrance, about 15 seconds. Add the mushrooms, zucchini, snow peas, onion, peppers, bean sprouts, and won bok, stir-frying for about 1 minute and keeping the vegetables crisp. Off heat, mix well, then add the pineapple and lychees. Add the chicken and set aside.

· Just before serving, add the dressing to the chicken and toss. Serve the salad on top of a bed of noodles and garnish with the chips.

- **Marinade**

  3 teaspoons oyster sauce

  1 teaspoon light soy sauce

  1 garlic clove, crushed

  ⅓ teaspoon hot pepper flakes

  1 teaspoon hoisin sauce

  Juice of 1 lime

  1 teaspoon rice wine

- **Chicken**

  1½ pounds boneless chicken breasts, cut into pieces

  1½ teaspoons peanut oil

ORIENTAL BARBECUED CHICKEN SALAD WITH PINEAPPLE AND LYCHEES

- **Salad**

  1½ teaspoons peanut oil

  2 teaspoons ginger

  2 teaspoons garlic

  3 shiitake mushrooms, cut into strips

  ¼ cup julienned zucchini

  ¼ cup snow peas

  ¼ sweet onion, sliced thin

  ¼ cup julienned yellow and red bell pepper

  ¼ cup bean sprouts

  ¼ cup shredded won bok (napa cabbage)

  3 teaspoons chopped ripe pineapple

  3 lychees, cut into pieces

  ¼ cup Roasted Cashew Dressing (page 165)

  2 cups cooked rice noodles

  ⅓ cup Wonton Chips (page 48)

  Serves 4

Vietnamese rice paper, or bahn trang, *can be found in many Asian food stores. It is important to roll these spring rolls tightly, because the stuffing has a tendency to loosen the wrapper. If you really like the flavor of basil, add a couple of whole basil leaves to the stuffing just before you roll the spring roll.*

Steamed Vietnamese Spring Rolls with Peanut Dip

. . . .

3 teaspoons peanut oil
2 teaspoons minced garlic
2 teaspoons minced fresh ginger
1 cup julienned carrots
1 cup julienned zucchini
1 cup julienned snow peas
1 cup bean sprouts
¼ cup thinly sliced basil leaves
2 cups Peanut Dip (page 170)
24 sheets rice paper
Pickled ginger, for serving

Makes 24 spring rolls

. . . .

· Carefully pour the peanut oil into a hot wok and fry the garlic and ginger until both release their fragrances. Add all the other vegetables and the basil, stir-frying until the vegetables are cooked but still crunchy, about half a minute. Add 1 cup of dip and mix well. Remove from heat and set aside until completely cool.

· Soften each rice paper by dipping it in lukewarm water. On a flat surface, place approximately 2 tablespoons of the vegetable mixture in the middle of each sheet, fold sides over, and roll it up tightly, like an egg roll.

· Place the spring rolls in a bamboo steamer lined with parchment and steam for 1 minute. You may have to do this in 2 or 3 batches. Carefully lift the spring rolls from the steamer, since they break easily.

· Serve warm or at room temperature, with Peanut Dip and pickled ginger on the side.

· Place the pork in the bowl of a food processor and chop. Add sherry, garlic, chili powder, coriander, red pepper, and salt and pepper to taste. Combine well.

· Peel and devein the shrimp and chop coarsely. Add to the pork mixture.

· Place 2 tablespoons of the pork mixture in the center of a wonton wrapper; fold wrapper up around the pork mixture, pinching it to create a cup for the mixture. Place in a steamer rack and steam over hot water for about 7 minutes. Remove from steamer and serve with dip.

In Honolulu, some Chinese cook-shops steam these suimai by the hundreds and sell them to people to reheat at home. They can be prepared in advance and kept in the refrigerator until you are ready to steam them.

STEAMED PORK AND SHRIMP SUIMAI WITH TERIYAKI DIP

. . . .

¼ pound pork butt or loin
¼ cup dry sherry
1½ teaspoons chopped garlic
½ teaspoon chili powder
¼ cup chopped fresh coriander
2 tablespoons diced red
    bell pepper
Salt and pepper
7 large shrimp
15 square wonton wrappers
Teriyaki Dip (page 181)

Serves 5

. . . .

You can make this salad using flank steak or tenderloin. I think that flank steak has more flavor and I also prefer its texture.

THAI BEEF SALAD WITH CRISP BASIL

. . . .

2 small heads red oak leaf lettuce

1 small head green oak leaf lettuce

½ red bell pepper, julienned

2 cups fresh bean sprouts

16 sprigs fresh coriander

2 garlic cloves, minced

1 teaspoon rice wine vinegar

⅓ cup reduced-sodium soy sauce

Juice of 2 limes

Salt and freshly ground pepper

1 pound flank steak

2 teaspoons vegetable oil

12 basil leaves

2 scallions, thinly sliced

2 small red chili peppers, diced

Serves 4–6

. . . .

· Prepare the grill.

· Wash salad greens. Place in a salad bowl and mix with the bell pepper, bean sprouts, and half the coriander. Reserve in a cool place.

· In a blender, combine the garlic, the leaves from half the coriander, the vinegar, soy sauce, and lime juice and blend thoroughly. Season with salt and pepper.

· Grill steak until medium rare, about 6 minutes. Allow to rest for 5 minutes, then slice thinly on a diagonal and reserve.

· Preheat a wok over high heat. Add the oil and stir-fry the basil, 2 leaves at a time, for a few seconds, then remove and drain on a paper towel. Add the garlic-coriander mixture and stir-fry for 2 minutes. Add the steak and stir-fry for 1 minute.

· Place steak slices on top of the salad mixture. Garnish with the basil, scallions, and chili and serve.

Pipikaula is a sort of Hawaiian beef jerky—dried, spiced beef used in salads or eaten alone. You can add additional flavors by brushing on some teriyaki sauce just before drying the beef, or adding freshly cracked black pepper and red pepper flakes. For this salad you can substitute a good store-bought beef jerky if you're not in the position to make your own. But it's worth the trouble, I assure you!

PIPIKAULA SALAD WITH HONEY-MUSTARD DRESSING

. . . .

- *Pipikaula*
  2 pounds lean flank steak
  Hawaiian sea salt or coarse salt
  ¼ cup water
  ⅓ cup light soy sauce
  1 tablespoon light brown sugar
  1 garlic clove, minced
  ½ teaspoon minced chili pepper
  1 small piece fresh ginger, minced
. . . .
- *Honey-Mustard Dressing*
  ⅓ cup white wine vinegar
  ¼ cup honey
  ⅓ teaspoon minced garlic
  ½ teaspoon yellow mustard seeds
  ½ teaspoon black mustard seeds
  ½ teaspoon dry mustard
  1 sage leaf, chopped fine
  Salt and pepper
  1 cup vegetable oil

  24 arugula leaves
  8 baby romaine lettuce leaves
  4 red oak leaf lettuce leaves

Serves 4

. . . .

· Cut the meat into long, thin slices about 1 inch wide. Sprinkle with salt on both sides.
· In a mixing bowl large enough to accommodate the meat strips, combine the water, soy sauce, brown sugar, garlic, chili pepper, and ginger, mix well, and add the meat. Toss the meat well to coat all sides evenly. Marinate the meat in the refrigerator for about 12 hours.
· When you are ready to dry the beef, drain the strips of the marinade; add any additional seasonings you want. Take out the racks in your oven, and attach the meat strips to one of the racks using paper clips or spring clips. Insert the rack into the top part of your oven, so that the meat strips hang down from rack. Heat at 150°F until they are dried, about 8 to 10 hours. (Once marinated, the meat strips can also be roasted or grilled and served on rice.) Set aside.
· In a large mixing bowl, combine the vinegar, honey, and minced garlic until well blended. Add the mustard seeds, dry mustard, sage, and salt and pepper to taste. Stir well. Slowly add the oil, a bit at a time, continuing to stir or whisk well.
· Combine the arugula, baby romaine, and red oak leaf lettuce with approximately 4 cups of the Pipikaula. Moisten with dressing, mix well, and serve.

- Combine the aku, ogo, salt, pepper flakes, scallion, onion, sesame oil, and ginger and marinate in the refrigerator for at least 15 minutes before serving.
- Note: Because Aku Poke is not cooked, only the best quality fish should be used. Look for red flesh that looks really fresh. Ahi can be substituted for aku, and you can also make this dish with tako (octopus).

Aku Poke—a local favorite—is a marinated fish dish that is a staple of luaus and is frequently among the assorted Hawaiian appetizers on a pupu platter. It is something like a ceviche, but since there is no lemon juice involved, the fish doesn't "cook." The aku—also known as skipjack tuna—caught in Hawaii during the summer weigh from fifteen to thirty pounds. They are a very popular fish and command a premium price in the market. According to legend, early settlers from Polynesia were caught in a storm that threatened to swamp their canoes. In response to their prayers, a school of aku appeared and calmed the waters. To honor the aku, it was forbidden (kapu) to eat the fish for a few days each year.

$\mathcal{A}$KU POKE

. . . .

2 pounds boneless aku or ahi,
    cut in ½-inch cubes
1 cup ogo (fresh seaweed),
    chopped
Hawaiian sea salt or coarse salt
1 teaspoon red pepper flakes
1 teaspoon chopped scallion
1 small sweet onion
1 teaspoon roasted sesame oil
1 teaspoon minced fresh ginger

Serves 4

. . . .

2

Soups

Some Hawaiians believe that this classic soup should contain macaroni, but I think the combination of sausage, ham hocks, and vegetables is enough. Like many soups, it is better if cooked a day or two in advance and then reheated slowly before serving. A good variation is to garnish the soup with some grated Cheddar cheese.

PORTUGUESE BEAN SOUP

. . . .

¼ cup olive oil

2 medium ham hocks

1½ cups cubed mild sausage, such as Portuguese sausage or Cajun sausage

3 medium potatoes, peeled and chopped

3 teaspoons chopped garlic

2 medium Maui onions, peeled and chopped

2 medium carrots, peeled and chopped

2 celery stalks, cleaned and chopped

4 cups cooked kidney beans

1 cup dry white wine

3 quarts chicken stock (page 214)

¼ cup tomato paste

1 bay leaf

Salt and pepper

3 medium tomatoes, peeled, seeded, and chopped

4 teaspoons chopped fresh parsley

Serves 6–8

. . . .

· In a large cooking pot, heat the olive oil and sauté the ham hocks slowly for about 8 minutes or until lightly browned. Add the sausage, potatoes, garlic, onions, carrots, and celery. Sauté for 2 minutes and add the kidney beans.

· Deglaze with the white wine, reduce liquid by two thirds, and add the stock. Bring to a boil and immediately reduce the heat to a simmer. Add the tomato paste and bay leaf, and season with salt and pepper. Simmer for between 20 and 25 minutes. Add the chopped tomatoes and cook for 5 minutes more.

· When ready to serve, remove the ham hocks from the soup, cut the meat into small cubes, and return to the soup. Serve in soup bowls and finish with chopped parsley.

Some of our customers love this soup so much that they order it by the quart to take home. The flavor of the curry paste takes a few minutes to develop, so don't add a lot in a hurry. Mark Miller, proprietor of the Coyote Cafe in Sante Fe, liked this soup so much he wanted to eat it for breakfast.

STEAMED FISH SOUP WITH COCONUT, BASIL, AND LEMON

. . . .

2 cups dry white wine

2 teaspoons chopped garlic

4 teaspoons julienned fresh ginger

4 cups clam juice or fish stock

4 cups coconut milk

3 stalks lemongrass, sliced

6 kaffir lime leaves, shredded
   very thinly

Salt

About 3 teaspoons red curry
   paste (page 216)

½ cup cornstarch

¼ cup water

Juice of 3 lemons

¼ cup julienned basil leaves

8 ounces snapper, cubed

8 medium shrimp, peeled
   and diced

Serves 8

. . . .

· In a large nonreactive pot combine the wine, garlic, and ginger and bring to a boil. Add the clam juice or fish stock and coconut milk and return to a boil. Add the lemongrass and lime leaves and season with salt to taste. Incorporate the curry paste. (The flavor takes a few minutes to develop; add more or less curry paste according to your taste.)

· Mix the cornstarch with the water and add this mixture to the soup. Cook for 5 minutes until it thickens. Add the lemon juice and half the basil and simmer the soup for a few more minutes.

· Steam the snapper for about 2 minutes and the shrimp for about 4.

· To serve, place a portion of snapper and a portion of shrimp in the bottom of each of 8 soup bowls. Fill each bowl with soup and garnish with the remaining basil.

- Peel the carrot, potato, and onion. Dice them, along with the celery and mushrooms, into ½-inch cubes. Cut the opakapaka into ½-inch dice as well. Set aside.
- Prepare a roux by melting the butter in a heavy pan and stirring in the flour. Cook over medium heat for 5 minutes, stirring constantly until it is a light brown paste, and set aside.
- In a large nonreactive saucepan, heat the olive oil and sauté the opakapaka very lightly for about 2 minutes, seasoning with salt and pepper to taste. Remove the fish with a slotted spoon and set aside.
- Sauté the vegetables in the remaining oil, beginning with the ginger and garlic, adding the potato, carrot, celery, onion, and mushrooms, one after the other in order, and cooking each addition for about 3 minutes.
- Add the wine and sherry and bring to a boil. Add the clams, cover the saucepan, and let cook for about 5 minutes. Remove the clams with a slotted spoon and scrape the clams from their shells; place the clams on the side and discard the shells.
- Add the fish stock and clam juice, bring to a boil, reduce the heat, and simmer for 5 minutes. Add the roux and the cream, stirring well to avoid lumps; let cook another 10 minutes. Return the clams and the opakapaka to the chowder, season with salt and pepper to taste, and finish with lemon juice. Serve the chowder in warmed soup bowls.

This hearty soup is wonderfully thick and full of chunky pieces of fish and vegetables. Serve it with Lavosh (page 195).

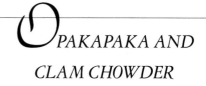

OPAKAPAKA AND CLAM CHOWDER

. . . .

1 medium carrot
1 medium potato
1 small onion
2 celery stalks
4 large button mushrooms
10 ounces opakapaka
   (pink snapper)
6 tablespoons (¾ stick) unsalted
   butter
¼ cup all-purpose flour
¼ cup olive oil
Salt and pepper
3 teaspoons chopped fresh ginger
2 teaspoons chopped garlic
½ cup dry white wine
½ cup dry sherry
30 clams
2 cups fish stock
2 cups clam juice
1 cup heavy cream
Juice of 1 lemon

Serves 6

. . . .

- With a cleaver cut the crabs into quarters. Chop the onion, carrot, celery, and tomatoes, and set aside until ready to use.
- Heat the vegetable oil in a large soup pot. Sauté the crab pieces for about 6 minutes, or until golden. Then add the onion, carrot, celery, and tomatoes, and sauté for 2 minutes more.
- Add the garlic, thyme, paprika, cayenne pepper, and tomato paste. Sauté for another 3 minutes, stirring often to prevent the tomato paste from burning. Deglaze with the white wine and add the fish stock, lemongrass, and lime leaves. Bring to a simmer and cook for about 20 minutes.
- Roast the chili peppers for 2 minutes until the skin becomes charred. Immediately place them in a small bowl or plastic bag and let sit, covered, for 10 minutes. The heat will steam off what remains of the skin on the peppers. With a paper towel remove the charred skin and seeds of the peppers. Combine the roasted chili peppers with the crème fraîche in a blender.
- With a slotted spoon remove the crabs from the stock and place in a blender. Blend the shells until they are thoroughly chopped and pour back into the stock. Add the fish sauce and bring to a boil. Simmer for 5 minutes.
- Pour the stock through a strainer, pressing down on the bits of shell to extract all the liquid. Discard the shells. Pour into soup bowls and finish with a dollop of pepper–crème fraîche mixture.

You can buy live blue crabs at many Asian markets. It is important to wear gloves when handling them because they are very active. If you are unable to find fresh crabs, they are also available frozen. Crème fraîche can be found in the dairy section of your market. In this recipe, you can substitute sour cream.

BLUE CRAB BISQUE WITH FILIPINO PEPPER CRÈME FRAICHE

. . . .

4 medium blue crabs, cleaned
1 medium onion
1 medium carrot
1 celery stalk
2 medium tomatoes
¼ cup vegetable oil
3 garlic cloves, minced
1 sprig fresh thyme
1 teaspoon paprika
Dash of cayenne pepper
½ cup tomato paste
½ cup dry white wine
2 quarts fish stock
2 stalks lemongrass, sliced
3 kaffir lime leaves, sliced
2 fresh red chili peppers
¼ cup crème fraîche
3 tablespoons fish sauce

Serves 4

. . . .

*This is a quick way to enjoy
real Pacific flavors. The green
papaya acts as a kind of starch
and thickens the soup naturally.
Cut the lemongrass and the kaffir
lime leaves as fine as possible
to release the maximum amount
of flavor.*

GREEN PAPAYA CHICKEN SOUP WITH CRAB MEAT

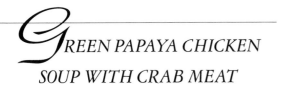

. . . .

1 teaspoon unsalted butter
1½ cups chopped chicken,
   in small pieces
½ Maui onion, chopped
2 medium green papayas, cubed
2 quarts chicken stock (page 214)
1 stalk lemongrass, finely sliced
2 teaspoons finely julienned
   kaffir lime leaf
1 cup crab meat
Salt and pepper

Serves 4–6

. . . .

· Melt the butter in a large pot over medium heat. Add the chicken and sauté gently until just cooked. Add the onion and papayas and sauté gently, making sure that the papayas don't change color. Add the stock, lemongrass, and lime leaf. Bring the mixture to a boil and let it simmer until the papaya is cooked, about 10 minutes.

· Add the crab meat, season to taste with salt and pepper, and simmer the soup until ready to serve.

· Note: If you can't find lemongrass or kaffir lime leaves, season the soup with lime juice instead. You can also substitute shrimp for the crab meat.

Lemon soup, a lemon-flavored
chicken stock, is simple to make
and very comforting when you
are not feeling well.

· In a skillet, heat the olive oil. When it is hot, add the onion
and chicken, and sauté until the chicken is cooked. Add the
ginger, cayenne pepper, chili powder, and paprika. Add
the barbecue sauce and mix well, then finish with the lemon
juice. Let the mixture cool.

· Before filling the wonton wrappers, dust your working table
with cornstarch to prevent the wrappers from sticking to the
table's surface. Place one wrapper on the table on the diagonal, moistening both sides lightly with water. Place filling in
the center of the wrapper and fold the dough into a triangle.
Seal both sides well by bringing the corners together. Wontons may be kept well covered in the refrigerator until ready
to use. When all the wontons are filled and sealed, blanch
them in boiling water for 1 minute, drain, and set aside.

· Wash the chicken bones thoroughly in cold water and drain.
In a large pot, combine the chicken bones and water and
bring to a boil. Ladle off any fat and foam that may accumu-
late at the top of the water. Add all other ingredients for soup,
reduce the heat, and simmer the stock for about 35 minutes.
Pass the stock through a strainer, return it to the pan, and
bring it back to a simmer. Season with salt and pepper.

· To serve the soup, place a portion of the garnishes in the bottom of each soup bowl. Add a chicken wonton to each bowl
and pour in the hot soup.

BARBECUED CHICKEN WONTON WITH LEMON SOUP

- *Barbecued Chicken Wonton*

  1 tablespoon olive oil

  ½ onion, chopped

  12 ounces boneless and skinless
  chicken, chopped

  2 teaspoons minced fresh ginger

  Pinch of cayenne pepper

  Dash of chili powder

  Pinch of paprika

  ½ cup barbecue sauce

  Juice of 1 lemon

  12 square wonton wrappers

- *Lemon Soup*

  1 pound chicken bones

  3 quarts water

  1 medium carrot

  1 medium onion

  3 stalks lemongrass, white ends
  slightly crushed

  6 kaffir lime leaves, thinly sliced

  ¼ cup sliced peeled fresh ginger

  Salt and pepper

- *Garnish*

  6 teaspoons black sesame seeds

  1 fresh red chili pepper, minced

  2 tablespoons chopped
  lemongrass

  ¼ cup bean sprouts

  4 tablespoons chopped basil

Serves 4

Koi tomatoes are well known in Hawaii, since they were the first greenhouse tomato to be introduced to the islands. They are consistent and very tasty. Tako is the Japanese word for octopus, and it is generally used on the islands.

COLD KOI TOMATO AND CUCUMBER SOUP WITH TAKO CEVICHE

. . . .

- *Soup*
  2 medium cucumbers, peeled
  4 ripe koi tomatoes
  ¼ medium carrot, peeled
  ½ celery stalk
  2 teaspoons minced garlic
  2 teaspoons Tabasco
  1 cup chicken stock (page 214)
  ½ cup olive oil
  Juice of 1 lime
  3 tablespoons sherry vinegar
  1 teaspoon mayonnaise
  Salt and pepper
  . . . .
- *Tako Ceviche*
  ¼ pound cooked tako legs,
    in ¼-inch-thick slices
    (see Note)
  Juice of 1 lime
  2 teaspoons chopped scallions
  1 teaspoon dry white wine
  1 ounce fresh red ogo or Japanese
    ogo nori seaweed, chopped
  Salt and pepper

  Serves 4–6

. . . .

· Slit the cucumbers lengthwise and remove the seeds. Using a paring knife, mark the blossom end of each tomato with a cross and place in boiling water for about 30 seconds. Remove and cool in ice water, then remove the skins. Cut in half and remove the seeds.
· Cut the cucumber, tomatoes, carrot, and celery into small dice. In a blender at medium speed, puree the vegetables, starting with the cucumber and then adding the tomatoes, celery, and carrot. Add the garlic, Tabasco, stock, olive oil, lime juice, vinegar, mayonnaise, and salt and pepper to taste. Place in refrigerator to chill well.
· In a small mixing bowl, combine the tako with the lime juice, scallions, wine, and seaweed. Season with salt and pepper to taste.
· When ready to serve, pour the chilled soup into bowls and place a dollop of the ceviche in the center of each bowl.
· Note: If using fresh tako, clean and steam for 3 minutes.

Bok choy, also known as Chinese white cabbage, is a relative of Chinese cabbage that is delicious raw, stir-fried, and steamed. Although the stock used in this soup is strong in character because it is made from the carcass of a marinated and roasted Chinese duck, the bok choy flavor predominates.

CHINESE DUCK SOUP WITH BOK CHOY

. . . .

- *Soup*

  Carcass of a Chinese-style duck, cut in pieces (page 215)

  1 cup diced carrots

  1 cup diced onion

  ½ cup shiitake mushroom stems

  6 fresh coriander sprigs

  2 garlic cloves, crushed

  1 teaspoon red pepper flakes

  ¼ cup sliced fresh ginger

  Salt and pepper

  . . . .

- *Garnishes*

  20 snow peas

  1 cup bok choy

  8 baby carrots

  8 medium shiitake mushrooms, sliced

  8 scallions, cut into julienne

  2 cups cooked Asian egg noodles

  2 duck breasts, cut in half

  2 duck legs, cut in half

  Serves 4

. . . .

· Place the duck carcass in a large pot and cover with water. Bring to a gentle boil.

· Add the carrots, onion, shiitake stems, coriander, and garlic. Cook over medium heat for about 1 hour, occasionally skimming off any fat that rises to the surface. Add the red pepper flakes and ginger and cook for 5 minutes more.

· Pass the soup through a strainer and return it to the pan, keeping it hot. Season with salt and pepper to taste.

· Steam all the vegetables for the garnish together. Meanwhile, place ½ cup of noodles in each of 4 soup plates. When the vegetables are cooked, divide them evenly among the plates, placing them on top of the noodles. Pour some of the soup over the vegetables and place ½ duck breast and ½ leg on each serving.

- Clean the watercress under cold water and chop into pieces. Peel the potatoes and dice. Peel the onion and slice lengthwise. Cut the pear into slices and cut the slices into julienne strips.
- Steam the abalone and cut into small cubes. If using canned abalone, steaming is not necessary.
- In a saucepan over medium heat, add the butter and sauté the potatoes, onion, and two thirds of the watercress. Let cook for about 5 minutes. Deglaze with the wine, reduce by one third, and add the stock. Bring to a boil and cook for about 10 minutes. Add the cream and cook for another 5 minutes.
- In a blender, puree the remaining watercress and the hot soup at medium speed until the mixture is smooth. Pour through a strainer and bring back to a boil. Season to taste with salt and pepper.
- Place the abalone and pears in the bottom of 4 soup bowls. Fill with hot soup and finish with a sour cream garnish.

I use wild watercress because it grows in a nearby pond on Kauai. If you are unable to find it, substitute cultivated watercress. Asian pears are yellow and about the size of a large apple. Abalone is raised commercially on the big island, and it also can be found in cans, usually from China.

WILD WATERCRESS SOUP WITH ASIAN PEAR AND ABALONE

2 bunches wild or cultivated
   watercress
2 medium potatoes
1 medium onion
1 Asian pear
6 ounces steamed fresh abalone,
   or ½ (15-ounce) can abalone
¼ cup (½ stick) unsalted butter
½ cup dry white wine
4 cups chicken stock (page 214)
2 cups heavy cream
Salt and pepper
4 teaspoons sour cream

Serves 4

3

Fish and Shellfish

This variation on classic fishcakes provides great flavor without deep-frying. Combining the shrimp with the fish makes for a smoother mixture than if fish alone is used, and it also results in a more interesting flavor. • The ogo, or fresh seaweed, comes from the Big Island. In the old days the locals would have their own spot where they would harvest their favorite seaweed. Because seaweed is now farmed, it is plentiful and easy to find. It has great flavor and is highly nutritious, and I believe that it will appear on more and more menus.

WOK-SEARED FISH AND SHRIMP CAKES WITH OGO-TOMATO RELISH

. . . .

1 pound snapper fillet, cubed

3 teaspoons chopped scallions

Salt and freshly ground
    black pepper

Dash of cayenne pepper

2 teaspoons chopped fresh ginger

1 teaspoon minced garlic

8 shrimp, peeled, deveined,
    and cubed

½ cup heavy cream

2 eggs, lightly beaten

3 teaspoons rice wine

2 cups bread crumbs

3 tablespoons vegetable oil

2½ cups Ogo-Tomato Relish
    (page 188)

Serves 4–6

. . . .

· In a blender combine the snapper, scallions, salt and pepper, cayenne pepper, ginger, garlic, and shrimp. Blend until the ingredients are a paste. Add the cream, eggs, and rice wine and blend once again.

· Transfer the mixture to a mixing bowl and form small cakes about 3 inches in diameter. Immediately coat the cakes with the crumbs and refrigerate until ready to cook.

· To cook, heat a wok or nonstick skillet over medium heat. Add the oil and sauté the fishcakes for about 2 minutes on each side. Remove from the skillet and place 2 fishcakes on each serving plate. Put a dollop of relish between them and serve immediately.

- Prepare the grill.
- In a shallow pan, combine olive oil, 2 sprigs of basil, and salt and pepper, and add the fish steaks. Marinate at least 15 minutes.
- Peel the papaya and discard the seeds. Cut flesh into small chunks. In a nonreactive saucepan, combine the shallots, mushrooms, wine, and papaya. Over medium heat, reduce the wine by two thirds, then add the cream. Reduce by two thirds again and whisk in the butter until the sauce thickens slightly. Pour the mixture into a blender, add the remaining basil, and blend until smooth. Adjust the seasoning if necessary.
- Grill the fish for about 2 minutes on each side, and serve with the sauce.

Ahi, or yellowfin tuna, is available in Hawaiian markets all year. It has the reputation of being dry, but when cooked on the pink side it is quite moist. I don't recommend using tombo ahi, or albacore tuna, which dries up faster during cooking. This recipe is great served over stir-fried vegetables.

GRILLED AHI WITH PAPAYA-BASIL SAUCE

. . . .

1 cup olive oil
5 sprigs fresh basil
Salt and white pepper
4 (7-ounce) ahi steaks
1 ripe but firm medium papaya
3 shallots, peeled and sliced
3 button mushrooms, sliced
1 cup dry white wine
½ cup heavy cream
4 tablespoons (½ stick) cold
    unsalted butter, cut into pieces

Serves 4–6

. . . .

- Mix the crab meat, shallots, ginger, coriander, eggs, cream, chili pepper, and tomatoes in a large bowl until well blended. Season to taste with salt and pepper.
- Roll out dough into 2 sheets the size of a ravioli tray, approximately 5 × 12 inches, allowing the bottom sheet to be a little larger than the top sheet. Place the top sheet of dough on the tray and fill each indentation with 1 to 2 tablespoons of stuffing. Cover with the bottom sheet and trim according to the ravioli tray's instructions. Dust lightly with semolina and set aside somewhere cool, or refrigerate while you make the sauce.
- Prepare the Crab-Lemongrass Sauce and keep warm.
- Bring a large quantity of water to a gentle boil in a large saucepan; add a pinch of salt and a little olive oil. Carefully add the ravioli and cook for 3 minutes. When cooked, remove with a slotted spoon and drain well. Heat butter in a skillet and sauté the ravioli briefly. Serve with the sauce.
- Note: If you don't have the time to make the egg noodle dough, you can use wonton skins or gyosa wrappers instead.

Samoan crabs, or mud crabs, are found mostly in muddy lagoons and rivers. They are used in Filipino and Thai cooking, though people throughout the Pacific Islands consider the meat to be a delicacy. They can be difficult to find, but you can also make this recipe with stone crabs or Dungeness crab.

SAMOAN CRAB MEAT RAVIOLI WITH CRAB-LEMONGRASS SAUCE

. . . .

1 pound crab meat, picked over
4 shallots, finely chopped
4 teaspoons minced fresh ginger
3 teaspoons finely chopped fresh coriander
2 eggs, lightly beaten
¼ cup heavy cream
1 fresh chili pepper, finely chopped
2 ripe medium plum tomatoes, finely chopped
Salt and pepper
1 pound Egg Noodle Dough (page 215)
Semolina for dusting

1 recipe Crab-Lemongrass Sauce (page 182)
Salt
Olive oil
2 tablespoons (¼ stick) unsalted butter

Serves 4–6

. . . .

Swordfish is the perfect fish to grill. I prefer a steak about 1½ inches thick, so the fish remains moist when cooked. This is a great dish for lunch—asparagus and sesame make a fantastic marriage of flavors, especially with the swordfish.

GRILLED SWORDFISH WITH ASPARAGUS-SESAME VINAIGRETTE

. . . .

4 (7-ounce) swordfish steaks

Salt and pepper

1 cup olive oil

32 pencil-thin asparagus spears

2 teaspoons red wine vinegar

1 teaspoon rice vinegar

¼ cup reduced-sodium soy sauce

2 teaspoons black sesame seeds

2 teaspoons white sesame seeds

6 julienned basil leaves

½ teaspoon minced garlic

3 teaspoons roasted sesame oil

1 cup bean sprouts

1 cup julienned snow peas

4 sprigs basil, for garnish

Serves 4

. . . .

· Marinate the swordfish in a mixture of salt, pepper, and ½ cup olive oil for at least 15 minutes.

· Blanch the asparagus for 3 minutes in boiling water with a pinch of salt. Remove and plunge into ice water. When the asparagus is cold, drain on a paper towel.

· Combine the vinegars, soy sauce, sesame seeds, basil, garlic, remaining olive oil, and sesame oil in a wide shallow mixing bowl. Mix well and add all the vegetables to the vinaigrette. Keep refrigerated until ready to serve.

· Prepare the grill. Drain the swordfish.

· Grill the fish for 3 minutes on each side or until medium–medium-rare and still moist on the inside.

· Divide the vegetables among 4 plates and place a swordfish steak on top. Garnish with a sprig of basil.

Many people are scared off when they see green curry—an incendiary combination of lemongrass, peppercorns, coriander seeds, and cumin—on the menu, but I love it. Serve with vegetables over brown rice.

WOK-SEARED SEA SCALLOPS WITH GREEN CURRY–COCONUT–BASIL SAUCE

- *Sauce*

  1 tablespoon tamarind paste

  ½ cup water

  ⅓ cup sliced fresh ginger

  1 teaspoon minced garlic

  2 cups coconut milk

  2 stalks lemongrass, cut in
    2-inch pieces

  6 kaffir lime leaves, finely
    julienned

  3 teaspoons green curry paste
    (page 216)

  1 teaspoon fish sauce

  6 basil leaves

  Juice of 1 lime

- *Scallops and
  Vegetables*

  3 tablespoons oil

  1½ pounds fresh sea scallops

  1 teaspoon minced garlic

  1 teaspoon minced fresh ginger

  1 cup sliced Japanese eggplant

  1½ cups snow peas, cleaned
    and strings removed

  ½ cup bean sprouts

  12 basil leaves, julienned

  1 teaspoon fish sauce

Serves 4

· Combine tamarind and water in a nonreactive saucepan and bring to a boil. When dissolved, add ginger and garlic, and bring to a boil again. Add coconut milk, lemongrass, lime leaves, curry paste, fish sauce, basil, and lime juice. Set aside in a warm place.

· Heat a wok or nonstick skillet over high heat. Add 1 tablespoon oil and sauté the scallops for about 2 minutes on each side. At the same time, heat another wok over high heat, add the remaining oil, and sauté the ginger and garlic for about 15 seconds. Add the eggplant and stir-fry until soft, about 3 minutes. Add the peas and stir-fry for another 2 minutes. Add the bean sprouts and basil and cook for 30 seconds. Add the fish sauce, stir throughly, and remove from heat.

· Divide the vegetables among 4 plates. Place the scallops over the vegetables and add a good dollop of sauce.

· Note: If you don't like the heat but enjoy the other flavors of this dish, you can make it without the green curry. And you can substitute shrimp for the scallops.

This is a truly international
dish—a combination of Japanese
tempura, a Chinese noodle cake,
and an Indian-inspired chutney.

TEMPURA-STYLE SOFT-SHELL CRABS WITH NOODLE CAKE AND TOMATO-GINGER-CORIANDER CHUTNEY

· In a medium mixing bowl, combine the flour and cornstarch. In a separate bowl, combine the eggs with the cold water and beat lightly. Add the eggs to the dry ingredients and stir briefly. The batter should not be worked too long; it doesn't matter if it is lumpy, since the lumps will fall off into the fat when the crabs are fried.

· In a wok, heat the oil until it is hot. Add the garlic and ginger and cook until golden. Add the zucchini, snow peas, won bok, mushrooms, and scallion and stir-fry until lightly cooked but still crisp.

· Add the noodles and mix well with the vegetables. Form the noodles into a cake and cook until the bottom turns golden. Turn the noodle cake over and cook until the other side turns golden.

· Fill a deep-fryer with the oil and heat it to 375°F. Dip the crabs into the batter and place them in the hot oil. Cook until they are crisp and golden, about 4 minutes. Drain on paper towels.

· Serve the crabs over the noodle cake and top with the chutney.

- **Tempura Batter**
  1 cup all-purpose flour
  ½ cup cornstarch
  2 eggs
  1¼ cups cold water

- **Noodle Cake**
  8 teaspoons oil
  1 teaspoon minced garlic
  1 teaspoon minced fresh ginger
  1 cup diced zucchini
  1 cup julienned snow peas
  1 cup shredded won bok
    (napa cabbage)
  1 cup shiitake mushrooms,
    sliced thin
  1 cup chopped scallion
  2 cups cooked Asian egg noodles

- **Crabs**
  Oil for deep-frying
  8 soft-shell crabs, cleaned
  Salt and pepper to taste

  1 recipe Tomato-Ginger-
    Coriander Chutney (page 172)

  Serves 4

- Clean the lettuces, separating a total of 8 whole leaves. Clean and slice the onion into ¼-inch slices. Trim the eggplant and cut into eight ¼-inch slices. Season the eggplant with salt and pepper to taste. Trim and cut the tomato into four ½-inch slices. Set aside.
- Heat the oil for deep-frying to 375°F. Dip each eggplant slice into the batter and deep-fry for approximately 2 minutes on each side or until golden. Set cooked slices on a paper towel to drain.
- Brush each fish steak with some olive oil and season both sides with salt and pepper. Sauté the fish, cooking only until medium-rare, about 2 minutes.
- Toast the sesame buns and spread with a small amount of mayonnaise. Add the lettuce, sliced tomato, onion, and basil. Add the fish and top with 2 slices of eggplant.
- Note: The ahi steaks can also be grilled. If you want more of an Asian flavor, you can marinate them in soy sauce for 15 minutes before cooking.

I consider this to be the perfect meatless sandwich. The basil makes it taste very fresh.

AHI SANDWICHES WITH TEMPURA EGGPLANT

. . . .

1 head baby leaf lettuce
1 head baby romaine lettuce
1 Maui onion
1 medium Italian eggplant
Salt and freshly ground pepper
1 large ripe tomato
4 (4-ounce) ahi (yellowfin tuna) steaks
Olive oil
Oil for deep-frying
2 cups tempura batter (page 85)
4 sesame buns or onion buns
Mayonnaise
8 basil leaves

Serves 4

. . . .

Kamanu, or rainbow runner, is known also as Hawaiian salmon. It is a very subtle fish. Mixed with spices and served with a gingery white pineapple relish, this fish will surprise your taste buds. If you can't find it, substitute salmon. • White pineapple are not as acidic as the common yellow variety, and the sugar content is a little higher, but you can substitute regular pineapple with little change in the flavor. • Oriental stores usually have supplies of dried seaweed, called nori or wakame, which can be used in place of fresh seaweed.

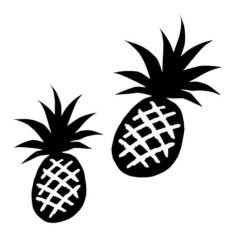

*W*OK-CHARRED KAMANU WITH WHITE PINEAPPLE RELISH

. . . .

1 medium pineapple, white
   if possible
1 fresh chili pepper
1 ounce ogo (fresh seaweed)
2 teaspoons chopped fresh ginger
2 pinches salt
1 tablespoon ground ginger
½ teaspoon red pepper flakes
½ teaspoon five-spice powder
2 teaspoons chopped fresh
   coriander
2 teaspoons toasted white
   sesame seeds
½ cup plus 1 tablespoon olive oil
2 teaspoons roasted sesame oil
Juice of 1 lime
4 (7-ounce) kamanu fillets

Serves 4–6

. . . .

· Peel the pineapple, trimming off all visible brown parts. Split the pineapple down the middle vertically and remove the core. Slice the pineapple, then dice into very small cubes.
· Chop the chili pepper finely and cut the ogo into small pieces. Add the chili pepper, ogo, fresh ginger, and salt to the pineapple.
· In a mixing bowl, combine the ground ginger, red pepper flakes, five-spice powder, coriander, sesame seeds, and 1 teaspoon salt. Add ½ cup olive oil, the sesame oil, and the lime juice. Marinate the fish in this mixture for at least 15 minutes.
· Slightly coat a wok with the remaining 1 tablespoon olive oil and heat until oil lightly smokes. Sauté the fish over medium heat for 4 minutes on each side.
· Place the fish on the center of a plate and put a strip of pineapple relish across the center.

· Season the fish with salt and pepper. Heat the olive oil in a nonstick skillet. Sauté the fish fillets for about 4 minutes on each side, until the fish is cooked medium-rare. Reserve on a plate and keep warm until ready to serve.

· Heat the fish stock or clam juice in a saucepan over high heat and reduce by one third. Reduce the heat and stir in the garlic, tomatoes, ginger, pepper, lime juice, turmeric, sesame oil, and seaweed and remove from the heat. Pour the sauce over the fish and serve at once.

Opakapaka, a pink snapper, has the reputation of being the best tasting of the snappers. It is a very delicate fish. If you can't find it, use any snapper. • When making this recipe, be sure to add the seaweed just before serving to obtain the maximum flavor. This dish is great served over angel hair pasta or stir-fried vegetables.

Seared Opakapaka with Tomato-Seaweed-Lime Broth

. . . .

• *Fish*

4 (8-ounce) opakapaka fillets
Salt and pepper
2 tablespoons olive oil

. . . .

• *Broth*

2 cups fish stock or clam juice
1 teaspoon minced garlic
3 cups diced tomatoes
1 teaspoon minced fresh ginger
Freshly ground black pepper
Juice of 2 limes
Dash of ground turmeric
2 teaspoons roasted sesame oil
2 cups chopped ogo, nori, or
    fresh Hawaiian seaweed

Serves 4

. . . .

This is one of the best-selling items at my restaurant. The Papaya-Basil Sauce is a kind of beurre blanc, and although we all have to be cautious about the amount of cream and butter we use, I believe that there is still a place for occasional richness. Sauces are the fun part of cooking!

SAUTEED CRAB CAKES WITH PAPAYA-BASIL SAUCE

. . . .

- *Crab Cakes*

  4 cups lump crab meat

  4 eggs

  Salt

  Cayenne pepper

  8 teaspoons minced fresh
     coriander

  4 teaspoons chopped red
     bell pepper

  2 teaspoons chopped garlic

  4 teaspoon chopped fresh ginger

  2–3 cups bread crumbs

  4 tablespoons olive oil

  Serves 4

. . . .

- *Papaya-Basil Sauce*

  1 cup dry white wine

  1 ripe medium papaya, diced

  1 shallot, diced

  ½ cup heavy cream

  ¾ cup (1½ sticks) unsalted
     butter, cut into pieces

  Salt and pepper

  2 teaspoons chopped fresh ginger

  Juice of 2 limes

  4 sprigs fresh basil

  Makes ⅔ cup

. . . .

· In a mixing bowl, combine the crab meat, eggs, salt, cayenne pepper, coriander, red pepper, garlic, and ginger. Blend well.

· With your hands, form the mixture into 8 cakes. Place the bread crumbs on a plate and dip the crab cakes in the crumbs so they are well coated.

· Heat the olive oil in a skillet, and when hot add the crab cakes and sauté until golden on both sides, about 2 minutes on each side.

· Pour some sauce on a plate, top with the crab cakes, and serve.

- *Papaya-Basil Sauce*

· In a nonreactive saucepan over medium heat, combine the wine, papaya, and shallot. Reduce the liquid by two thirds, then add the cream and reduce again by two thirds. Slowly whisk in the butter, incorporating each piece before adding another. Season with salt, pepper, ginger, and lime juice. Transfer the mixture to a blender and blend until the ingredients are well combined.

· Pour the sauce into a bowl and add the basil. Allow it to infuse for at least 20 minutes before serving.

Ulua is considered to be the smartest fish in the waters by many Hawaiian fishermen, and it is one of my favorites. Weighing more than ten pounds, it is caught in both deep and shallow waters. This dish combines elements of East and West. The tomato paste in the sauce acts as a thickener and gives the dish a rich flavor. Papio or pompano can be substituted for the ulua.

Seared Ulua with Mushroom Cannelloni and Sweet Ama Ebi Sauce

. . . .

- *Cannelloni*

  3 teaspoons olive oil

  2 teaspoons minced fresh garlic

  2 cups sliced shiitake mushrooms

  2 cups fresh chanterelle
  mushrooms

  3 teaspoons sherry vinegar

  1/3 cup heavy cream

  Salt and pepper

  4 cooked 4 × 6-inch square pasta
  sheets (see recipe for Egg
  Noodle Dough, page 215)

  8 teaspoons grated Parmesan
  cheese (optional)

. . . .

- *Ulua*

  4 (7-ounce) ulua fillets

  Salt, pepper, and ground ginger
  to taste

  4 teaspoons roasted sesame oil

  2 cups Sweet Ama Ebi Sauce
  (page 183)

  Serves 4

. . . .

- Preheat oven to 350°F.
- Heat the olive oil in a sauté pan over medium heat, and when it is hot, add the garlic and mushrooms and sauté for a few seconds. Reduce the heat and add the vinegar and cream. Let the mixture cook until the cream reduces slightly. Season to taste with salt and pepper.
- Place one fourth of the mushroom mixture and 1 teaspoon of cheese, if using, on each of the 4 pasta sheets and roll them each into a 1-inch cylinder. Place seam side down on a deep serving dish. Top with remaining cheese and bake for 5 minutes. Keep warm.
- Season the fish fillets with the salt, pepper, and ginger.
- Heat the oil in a large skillet, and when it is hot, sauté the fish until golden on each side, about 3 minutes on each side.
- To serve, place 1 cannelloni cut into 2 pieces in each of 4 soup plates. Put an ulua fillet on top of the cannelloni and top with the Sweet Ama Ebi Sauce.

· In a nonreactive saucepan over medium heat, combine the pineapple, stock, and ginger. Bring slowly to a boil and simmer for about 10 minutes. Add rum, then puree the mixture in a blender. Pass the sauce through a fine strainer and add the sage. Season with salt and pepper and reserve until needed.

· Prepare the grill. Season the fillets, brush with olive oil, and grill for 3 minutes on each side.

· Remove the sage from the sauce. Place 1 cup of the sauce on each of 4 dinner plates, and place 1 fillet on top. Serve immediately.

Nairagi is more commonly known as striped marlin. It is a very tender fish and is considered by many to be the best marlin for eating. If you can't find it, use mako shark.

• Pineapple and rum make a wonderful cocktail, so I thought it would be fun to make a sauce that resembled it. The addition of sage brings a lot of flavor to the whole composition. This sauce is very simple to prepare and includes no cream, butter, or oil, reflecting both the Asian influence and the trend today to reduce the amount of fat in our diets.

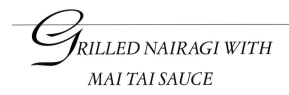

GRILLED NAIRAGI WITH MAI TAI SAUCE

. . . .

• *Mai Tai Sauce*

1 cup ripe pineapple cubes

3 cups chicken stock (page 214)

2 teaspoons chopped fresh ginger

3 tablespoons dark rum,
preferably Hana Bay

5 sprigs fresh sage

Salt and pepper

. . . .

• *Fish*

4 (8-ounce) nairagi fillets

Salt and pepper

⅓ cup olive oil

Serves 4

. . . .

This dish is usually served as an appetizer, but it is also a great main course. It is delicious served over stir-fried vegetables. You'll need a bamboo steaming basket to make it the authentic way, but many Asian stores stock them.

STEAMED RICE PAPER–WRAPPED SALMON WITH CORIANDER PESTO

. . . .

1 pound salmon fillet

½ cup dry sherry

Salt and pepper

2 tablespoons minced fresh ginger

1 teaspoon pastis or fish sauce

1 tablespoon lemon juice

2 tablespoons chopped
   macadamia nuts

1 tablespoon chopped garlic

2 tablespoons chopped
   fresh coriander

24 sprigs fresh coriander, rinsed
   clean

2 tablespoons olive oil

12 round 10-inch sheets
   rice paper

Serves 4

. . . .

· Cut the salmon into 12 equal pieces. In a shallow, nonreactive pan, combine the salmon, sherry, salt and pepper, ginger, and pastis. Marinate the fish 1 hour. Drain.

· In a blender, combine the lemon juice and macadamia nuts and process until you obtain a light paste. Add the garlic and coriander, blending continuously. Increase the speed and add the olive oil.

· Moisten one rice paper at a time with warm water and let dry for half a minute before rolling. Place 1 teaspoon of the pesto in the center of each wrapper and place a piece of marinated salmon on top. Place 2 sprigs of coriander on top of the salmon. Fold the paper closest to you over the salmon, then fold the ends into the center and roll away from you. Repeat until all ingredients have been used.

· Place the rolls in a bamboo steamer over boiling water and steam for about 2 minutes. If there is any pesto left over, use it to garnish the rolls.

Kajiki, or Pacific blue marlin, is a firm fish with a mild flavor that can support a strong sauce or hearty relish. It was feared by Hawaiian fishermen because its heavy bill could easily pierce a traditional fishing canoe. If you can't find kajiki, use swordfish or halibut.
• This recipe calls for Portuguese sausage; if it isn't available, substitute any other mildly spicy sausage you like, such as Thai or Cajun sausage.

GRILLED KAJIKI WITH SAUSAGE AND GRILLED CORN RELISH

. . . .

4 (7-ounce) kajiki fillets
Salt and pepper
¾ cup olive oil
4 teaspoons chopped fresh
    oregano, or 1 teaspoon dried
2 ears of corn, in husk
12 ounces Portuguese sausage
    (linguica)
1 red bell pepper
2 shallots
1 teaspoon minced garlic
1 teaspoon chili powder
Pinch of cayenne pepper
2 teaspoons chopped fresh sage,
    or 1 teaspoon dried
1 tablespoon red wine vinegar

Serves 4–6

. . . .

· Prepare the grill.
· In a shallow, nonreactive pan, marinate the fish with salt, pepper, ½ cup olive oil, and 2 teaspoons of the oregano for at least 15 minutes. Drain.
· Peel down husks from corn and remove silks. Pull husks back up over corn and twist closed. Grill the corn until the husks are charred. Let cool slightly. When lukewarm, peel off the husks and discard. Cut the kernels from the cob with a knife and set aside.
· Meanwhile, grill the sausage until cooked through, about 10 minutes. Let cool slightly. When lukewarm, chop into small pieces about the same size as the corn kernels. Finely chop the red pepper and shallots.
· In a medium mixing bowl, combine the corn, sausage, red pepper, shallots, garlic, chili powder, cayenne pepper, sage, and remaining oregano. Add the remaining olive oil and the vinegar and mix well.
· Coat the fish with olive oil and grill for 3 minutes on each side. Place the relish on a plate and serve the fish on top.

Kamaaina *means "old timer," or a longtime Hawaiian resident. Served with steamed white or brown rice, this simple dish is a treat for seafood lovers. The peppery flavor of the fried ginger marries beautifully with the scallion and fresh coriander. The only secret to making this dish is to heat the oil to very hot and pour it over the fish just when you are ready to serve it.*

STEAMED HAWAIIAN SNAPPER, "KAMAAINA" STYLE

. . . .

1 whole snapper, 1 to 1½
    pounds, scaled and cleaned
⅓ cup finely julienned
    fresh ginger
2 cups julienned shiitake
    mushrooms
1 teaspoon white sesame seeds
¼ cup plus 2 tablespoons
    peanut oil
1 cup julienned scallions
¼ cup chopped fresh coriander
½ cup dark soy sauce
3 teaspoons roasted sesame oil

Serves 4

. . . .

· Heat water in a wok in which a bamboo steamer can be placed. Place the whole fish in a bamboo steamer, and steam for approximately 30 minutes, or until the meat close to the center bone is cooked.

· Place the fish on a serving plate and sprinkle the julienned ginger on top.

· In a skillet, sauté the mushrooms and sesame seeds in 2 tablespoons of the peanut oil for just 2 minutes. Spoon this mixture on top of the fish as well.

· Sprinkle on the scallions and coriander, and pour the soy sauce evenly over the fish.

· In a small saucepan, heat the remaining peanut oil and the sesame oil until smoking, and pour carefully over the fish. Serve immediately.

Kajiki, commonly known as Pacific blue marlin, is a member of the billfish family and is available during summer and fall. Its high fat content makes it perfect for grilling, and it is often substituted for tuna in sashimi. A kamado is a Japanese smoker; any other type of smoker can be used in this recipe. Fruit woods, such as pear, guava, or pecan, add a nice flavor.

KAMADO-SMOKED PEPPERED KAJIKI WITH GREEN CURRY RATATOUILLE

. . . .

½ cup chopped fresh sage
½ cup chopped fresh oregano
¼ cup olive oil
4 (7-ounce) kajiki pieces
Salt and cracked black
   peppercorns
Green Curry Ratatouille
   (page 153)

Serves 4

. . . .

· In a small bowl, combine the herbs and add the olive oil. Mix well and set aside.
· Prepare the smoker.
· Season the fish with salt and cracked black pepper. Brush the fish with the olive oil mixture and place fish in the smoker. Smoke the fish for 10 minutes. It should be on the moist side.
· Serve with ratatouille.

$\mathcal{S}$ TEAMED HAWAIIAN LOBSTER TAIL WITH VEGETABLES IN YELLOW CURRY AND LIME SAUCE

· Make the sauce. In a saucepan, heat the sake, ginger, garlic, and lemongrass over high heat and reduce liquid by one third. Add stock and cream, then reduce again by one third, add lime juice and curry powder, and simmer briefly. Set aside.

· Place lobster tails in a large bamboo steamer lined with ti leaves along with lemongrass. Sprinkle with lime juice, then steam for about 4 minutes. Place vegetables in steamer along with lobster and steam another 4 minutes.

· To serve, place a spoonful of the vegetables in the center of a plate; slice the steamed lobster tails in half lengthwise and place on top of steamed vegetables. Serve with the Yellow Curry and Lime Sauce.

. . . .

4 lobster tails, each approximately
    ¾ pound
3 ti leaves
3 stalks lemongrass
Juice of 2 limes
½ cup sliced yellow squash,
    in julienne strips
½ cup sliced zucchini,
    in julienne strips
½ cup sliced carrot, in
    julienne strips
12 snow peas, cut into
    julienne strips
2 fresh red chili peppers, sliced
4 baby Japanese eggplant, diced
    into ½-inch cubes

Serves 4

. . . .

• *Yellow Curry and Lime Sauce*

1 cup sake
1 teaspoon chopped fresh ginger
1 teaspoon chopped garlic
1 stalk lemongrass, thinly sliced
1 cup lobster stock
⅔ cup heavy cream
Juice of 1 lime
2 teaspoons yellow curry powder

Makes 1 cup

. . . .

Cooking shabu-shabu style—dipping morsels of meat and vegetables in hot broth with chopsticks—is very popular in Japanese restaurants. The term shabu-shabu *comes from the sound these morsels make as they cook. Although the mahi-mahi in this recipe is not cooked shabu-shabu style, it makes a great sound when served on a sizzling platter. And the sauce that accompanies it is a classic shabu-shabu dipping sauce.*

*S*IZZLING GINGER MAHI-MAHI WITH SHABU DIPPING SAUCE

. . . .

¼ cup roasted sesame oil

½ cup peanut oil

1 pound boneless mahi-mahi, cut into strips

1 Maui or other sweet onion, sliced very thin

½ cup julienned fresh ginger

2 teaspoon minced fresh red chili pepper

Salt

Juice of 2 limes

½ cup Shabu Dipping Sauce (page 187)

Serves 4

. . . .

· Place an ovenproof platter in a 400°F oven for about 30 minutes.

· Place a wok over high heat and add the sesame and peanut oils. When the oils are very hot, add the fish and stir-fry until it turns a golden color, about 3 minutes.

· Add the onion and ginger and stir-fry for another minute. Add the chili pepper and season with salt. Stir-fry for just a few seconds, then transfer to the sizzling hot serving platter. Sprinkle the lime juice over the top. Serve with the dipping sauce.

· Note: It is better to undercook the mahi-mahi slightly because it will cook a little more on the hot platter.

· Combine the rice wine, basil, chili pepper, lemon juice, and salt in a nonreactive dish. Add the fish fillets and marinate for at least 20 minutes. Drain.

· Heat the oil in a deep saucepan to 375°F. Dredge the fish in the flour and deep-fry until golden, about 4 minutes. Keep warm.

· In a medium saucepan, heat the oil over medium heat and sauté the onion and garlic until translucent. Add the bell peppers and sauté for 1 minute, taking care that they do not take on any color. Add the ginger and wine and let reduce for about 1 minute. Add the stock and passion fruit juice, bring to a boil, and let simmer for about 2 minutes. Add the fish sauce and soy sauce.

· Mix the cornstarch with some cold water. Add to the sauce mixture and let simmer for about 2 minutes, until the sauce thickens and coats the back of a spoon. Serve over the sea bass.

The Hawaiian name for black sea bass is hapu'upu'u. It is very popular with the Chinese population. Lilikoi is the Hawaiian word for passion fruit.

LILIKOI-GINGER SWEET-AND-SOUR BLACK SEA BASS

. . . .

- *Fish*

  1 cup rice wine

  ½ cup chopped fresh basil

  2 teaspoons minced fresh red
     chili pepper

  Juice of 2 lemons

  Salt

  1½ pounds black sea bass fillets,
     cut in 3-inch strips

  Oil for deep-frying

  1½ cups all-purpose flour

. . . .

- *Lilikoi-Ginger
  Sweet-and-Sour Sauce*

  3 tablespoons vegetable oil

  ½ large onion, chopped

  1 teaspoon minced garlic

  ½ green bell pepper, diced

  ½ red bell pepper, diced

  3 tablespoon minced fresh ginger

  2 teaspoon rice wine

  ⅓ cup chicken stock (page 214)

  1 cup passion fruit (lilikoi) juice

  2 teaspoons fish sauce

  2 tablespoons reduced-sodium
     soy sauce

  2 tablespoons cornstarch

Serves 4

. . . .

Ono, a close relative of the mackerel, cooks very fast and becomes dry if left on the grill too long. I prefer to grill it over aromatic wood, such as eucalyptus or kiawe. Use a mackerel if you can't find ono. • Mangos are indigenous to Southeast Asia and are excellent sources of vitamin B. If mangos are unavailable, a papaya salsa can be served.

$\mathcal{W}$OOD-GRILLED ONO WITH MANGO CHUTNEY

- *Fish*

  4 (7-ounce) ono fillets
  Salt and pepper
  Olive oil, for brushing on fish

  Serves 4

- *Mango Chutney*

  3 cups diced mango
  ¼ cup diced fresh ginger
  2 teaspoons minced garlic
  Pinch of salt
  ¼ cup white wine vinegar
  1 cup Hawaiian sugar
  ¾ cup diced sweet onion, such as
     Maui or Vidalia
  2 fresh chili peppers, diced
  2 teaspoons honey, clove
     if possible

  Makes 1½ cups

· Prepare the grill.
· Season the fish with salt and pepper. Brush it with olive oil and grill it over a medium fire for 3 minutes on each side. Serve with the chutney.

- *Mango Chutney*

· Season the mango with the ginger, garlic, and salt and set aside.
· Combine the vinegar and sugar in a saucepan and bring to a boil. Add the mango, onion, chili peppers, and honey and simmer for about 45 minutes, or until the chutney reaches the desired consistency. I like the mango pieces to remain a little firm. Store in the refrigerator.

Kumu is a great-tasting reef fish, sometimes called goat fish, that is very expensive and hard to find in the market—the local fishermen usually keep it for themselves. One of my customers likes kumu so much that he has formed the "Kumu Club." When he visits Kauai, I have to talk some of the fishermen into selling me some kumu. The fish average between one and two pounds, with the fillets weighing seven to eight ounces. You can use red snapper if kumu is not available. Serve over stir-fried vegetables.

Steamed Kumu with Lemongrass–Shiitake Broth

- *Fish*

  4 (7-ounce) kumu fillets,
    with skin
  Salt and pepper
  2 stalks lemongrass, split in half

- *Broth*

  1 cup strong fish stock or
    clam juice
  3 kaffir lime leaves, finely
    shredded
  1 stalk lemongrass, cut into
    small pieces
  15 shiitake mushrooms, sliced
  1 medium piece fresh ginger,
    smashed
  Dash of red pepper flakes

  12 sprigs fresh coriander,
    for garnish

Serves 4

· Season the fish with salt and pepper.
· Place a small amount of water in a wok and bring it to a boil. Place a bamboo steamer in the wok and put the lemongrass in the steamer, topped by the fish. Steam the fish for about 8 minutes or until done.
· Meanwhile, in a saucepan combine the stock, lime leaves, lemongrass, mushrooms, ginger, and red pepper flakes. Simmer the mixture for about 5 minutes.
· To serve, place the vegetables on individual plates. Put fish fillets on top. Top each serving with the broth and garnish with coriander.

- Season the fish with the cayenne pepper, chili pepper, and salt. Squeeze on the lemon juice, and cover with the coriander leaves.
- Moisten 1 piece of rice paper with warm water. Place half a sheet of nori on the rice paper, add a fish piece, fold in the ends, and roll up tightly. Continue until all ingredients have been used.
- Heat the peanut oil in a wok over medium high and sauté the fish packages until golden brown and cooked through, about 3 minutes. Drain on paper towels.
- To serve, place 3 tablespoons of the relish in the center of each plate and arrange 3 "firecrackers" around it.

- *Papaya-Pineapple Relish*
- In a large mixing bowl, combine the papaya, pineapple, onion, chili peppers, mint, and garlic. Mix well and add the vinegar and oil. Season to taste with salt. Refrigerate for at least 15 minutes before serving. Serve at room temperature.

This dish, which can be served as an appetizer or as a main course, combines the sharpness of citrus with the heat of chili peppers. The rice paper becomes crisp when sautéed. You taste the lemon flavor first, but it soon disappears under the heat of the peppers!

FIRECRACKER ONO WITH SPICY PAPAYA-PINEAPPLE RELISH

. . . .

1½ pounds ono (wahoo) fillets,
    cut into twelve 1 × 3-inch strips
2 pinches cayenne pepper
1 teaspoon minced fresh red
    chili pepper
Salt
Juice of 2 lemons
¼ bunch fresh coriander
12 10-inch sheets rice paper
6 sheets roasted nori
½ cup peanut oil

Serves 4

. . . .

- *Papaya-Pineapple Relish*
    1 cup peeled and diced ripe
        medium papaya
    1 cup diced pineapple
    3 tablespoons diced onion
    3 fresh red chili peppers, diced
    1 tablespoon chopped fresh mint
    1 teaspoon minced garlic
    2 teaspoons rice wine vinegar
    2 tablespoons olive oil
    Salt

Makes 2½ cups

. . . .

*Mahi-mahi, or dolphinfish, are
beautiful to look at and to eat.
Blue and yellow in color, their flesh
tastes almost sweet. On the mainland, the best mahi-mahi is sure to
come from Hawaii—frozen mahi-
mahi from Taiwan and Latin
America just doesn't compare.*

SEARED MAHI-MAHI WITH A GARLIC-SESAME CRUST AND ASPARAGUS RELISH

- *Fish*

  4 (7-ounce) mahi-mahi fillets

  Salt and freshly ground pepper

  1½ cups white sesame seeds

  5 teaspoons chopped garlic

  ½ cup (1 stick) unsalted
    butter, softened

  3 tablespoons olive oil

  Serves 4

- *Asparagus Relish*

  24 pencil-thin asparagus spears,
    steamed or blanched

  1 teaspoon chopped garlic

  4 teaspoons chopped
    pickled ginger

  1 medium tomato, peeled,
    seeded, and diced

  1 yellow bell pepper, cleaned
    and diced

  Salt and freshly ground white
    pepper

  1 cup Black Sesame Dressing
    (page 164)

  4 basil sprigs, for garnish

  Serves 4

· Season each fish fillet with salt and pepper and set aside.

· Mix the sesame seeds and garlic into the softened butter, adding salt and pepper to taste. Spread top of the fish fillets with the mixture to form a ¼-inch crust.

· Pour the olive oil into a heated wok or nonstick skillet. When the oil is hot, sear each fillet on both sides and top and bottom. Be careful not to overcook the fish. When cooked, in about 1 minute, transfer to a warm plate, garnish with basil, and serve with Asparagus Relish.

- *Asparagus Relish*

· Combine the asparagus, garlic, ginger, tomato, bell pepper, salt and pepper, and Black Sesame Dressing in a medium mixing bowl, stirring well. Refrigerate until ready to use.

An imu is an underground oven that has a long history in Hawaii. A shallow hole in the ground is lined with carefully chosen lava rock, and a fire is set over it until the rock is red-hot. Banana leaves are placed over the rocks, food is set on the leaves, and the whole thing is covered completely and left to steam. The food cooked in an imu becomes incredibly tender and flavorful.
• You can reproduce the effect of imu cooking in your kitchen using the following recipe. If you can't get onaga, use any small snapper.

IMU-BAKED ONAGA WITH HAWAIIAN SALT

. . . .

2 banana leaves, if available
1 (2-pound) whole onaga
   (long-tailed red snapper)
Salt and pepper
6 Thai basil leaves
1 teaspoon minced garlic
1 teaspoon minced fresh ginger
1 stalk lemongrass, crushed
5 sprigs fresh coriander
2 teaspoons Hawaiian sea salt
1 pinch turmeric
1 cup ogo (fresh seaweed)
2 kaffir lime leaves, cut into
   julienne strips
½ cup coconut milk
¼ teaspoon liquid smoke
1 lime, thinly sliced
Oriental Dip (page 52)

Serves 4–6

. . . .

· If using banana leaves, soften the leaves over a gas flame. With tongs, hold each leaf over a medium flame, turning it until the entire leaf has been exposed to the flame. This will make the leaf very pliable and easy to work with. (If banana leaves are not available, aluminum foil or parchment paper are the best substitutes.)
· Preheat the oven to 350°F.
· Clean and fillet the fish, removing scales, fins, and bones. Season the fish on the skin side with salt and pepper. Place the basil, garlic, and ginger on the filleted side.
· Place the fish in the center of the banana leaf (or foil or parchment paper) in a baking dish and add the lemongrass. Top the fish with the coriander and salt, then add the turmeric, ogo, lime leaves, coconut milk, and liquid smoke. Place the lime slices on top.
· Fold the banana leaf over the fish, making sure it is completely enclosed. Bake for about 30 minutes. Remove from the oven and serve with the dip.

· Heat some water in a wok. Place the fish in a deep platter that will fit in a bamboo steamer. Add the sherry, ginger, black beans, chili pepper, and leek. Place in the steamer and steam for about 8 minutes, or until the fish is cooked through. In the meantime, heat the sesame oil in a small saucepan.

· Remove the platter from the steamer and pour the soy sauce and scallions over the fish.

· Pour hot sesame oil over the fish. Serve the fish directly from the platter.

Monchong is from the same family as the bigscale pomfret, another favorite fish among the Chinese population in Hawaii. The monchong is extremely tender, and the addition of the black beans, hot sesame oil, and soy sauce results in an explosion of flavors. This preparation will also work well with halibut.

STEAMED MONCHONG, ORIENTAL STYLE

. . . .

1 (1-pound) monchong fillet,
    with skin
1 cup dry sherry
½ cup julienned fresh ginger
½ cup fermented black beans,
    chopped
1 teaspoon red chili pepper,
    diced
1 cup julienned leek, white
    part only
3 teaspoons roasted sesame oil
½ cup dark soy sauce
½ cup julienned scallions

Serves 4

. . . .

Opah, also called moonfish, weighs up to 80 pounds. The belly is the fattier part, so that is what is used for sashimi. If you can't find opah, use turbot or halibut.

SEARED OPAH WITH VEGETABLE RELISH AND ANNATTO VINAIGRETTE

. . . .

- *Fish*
  4 (7-ounce) opah pieces
  Salt and pepper
  4 teaspoons olive oil
  1 Deep-Fried Lotus Root
     (page 150)

Serves 4

. . . .

- *Vegetable Relish*
  2 Japanese eggplants
  2 medium tomatoes, peeled,
     seeded, and cubed
  ½ medium avocado, diced
  ½ red bell pepper, cut in
     julienne strips
  1 teaspoon chopped garlic
  ⅔ cup Annatto Vinaigrette
     (page 188)

Makes 3 cups

. . . .

· Season the fish with salt and pepper. Put the oil in a heated wok or nonstick skillet and sauté the seasoned fish until medium-rare, about 6 minutes.
· To serve, place a large spoonful of Vegetable Relish in the middle of each plate and top with a fillet. Garnish with Deep-Fried Lotus Root.

- *Vegetable Relish*
· Cut the eggplant into ½-inch dice and stir-fry in a wok over medium-high heat until soft.
· In a bowl, mix the tomatoes, avocado, red pepper, and garlic. Add the eggplant and dressing. Set aside for at least 5 minutes, until ready to serve.

Yellowfin tuna is most abundant in summer. The quality of the fish depends a great deal on how it is harvested. Because of its high fat content, sashimi-quality yellowfin is the most expensive. As a substitute, regular tuna works well in recipes using a vinaigrette or in which the fish has been coated with spices.

· Combine the oil and herbs in a bowl. Season the fish with the salt and pepper. Cover the fish with the olive oil–herb mixture and marinate for at least 30 minutes.

· Prepare the grill.

· Grill the fish over medium heat for approximately 2 minutes on each side, depending on the quality and freshness of the fish. Tuna is best medium-rare.

· Serve with Garlic Chips and Avocado Relish.

● *Garlic Chips*

· Heat oil in a deep saucepan to 375°F. Slice the garlic cloves into the thinnest possible slices. Deep-fry until they turn light brown, approximately 2 minutes. Drain on paper towels and season with salt.

*B*ARBECUED YELLOWFIN TUNA WITH GARLIC CHIPS AND AVOCADO RELISH

. . . .

● *Fish*
½ cup olive oil
½ cup shredded basil leaves
¼ cup shredded fresh coriander
4 (7-ounce) yellowfin tuna steaks
Salt and freshly ground
   black pepper

. . . .

● *Garlic Chips*
Oil for deep-frying
8 garlic cloves, peeled
Salt

1¾ cups Avocado Relish
   (page 179)

Serves 4

. . . .

4

Meat and Poultry

Laulau is a classic Hawaiian dish in which a bundle of fish, beef, pork, or chicken is wrapped in leaves and steamed. It is real Hawaiian home cooking and a fixture at luaus, and is also a great dish for a buffet. Some make laulau with only one main ingredient, but I really like the contrast of flavors. • Papio is the smaller ulua, which usually weigh ten pounds or less. If you can't find it, use pompano, pomfret, or sea bream. If luau leaves are unavailable, spinach can be used, in which case the steaming time should be about 45 minutes. Check the level of the water every so often—this is a must in Hawaiian cooking, especially during luau.

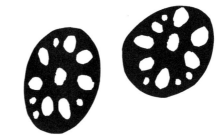

CHICKEN, PAPIO, AND PORK LAULAU

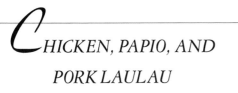

. . . .

9 ounces papio fillet

14 ounces pork butt, cut into
   1-inch cubes

8 ti leaves

20 luau leaves, washed and dried,
   or two bunches spinach,
   blanched

4 chicken thighs, boned

1 tablespoon Hawaiian sea salt

Serves 4

. . . .

· Cut the fish and pork into equal portions. Using 2 ti leaves for each serving, lay the leaves in a cross pattern on a work surface. Place 5 luau leaves on each of these 4 crosses. Season the fish, pork, and chicken with the Hawaiian salt and place an equal amount of meat and fish in the center of each leaf arrangement. Fold the leaves over the meat and fish and wrap each package tightly, securing with butcher string.

· Steam for 3 to 4 hours in a bamboo steamer set inside a wok. Remove and serve on plates, letting each person open a package.

- Heat oil to 375°F. Split noodles apart and deep-fry until they puff up, about 10 seconds. Remove from the oil and drain. Set aside.
- In a large wok, heat the peanut oil. When it is very hot, add the garlic and ginger and stir for just a few seconds. Add the steak and stir-fry until medium-rare, about 2 minutes.
- Add the broccoli, red pepper, bean sprouts, and snow peas and stir-fry for 2 minutes. Add the wine, oyster sauce, soy sauce, and red pepper flakes and mix well.
- Serve the meat and vegetables over the deep-fried noodles.

Also called bean threads, cellophane noodles are available in most Asian markets. In this recipe they are added a few at a time to the hot oil, and like magic they increase in volume three or four times.

STIR-FRIED SPICY FLANK STEAK WITH CELLOPHANE NOODLES

. . . .

- *Cellophane Noodles*

  Oil for deep-frying

  12 ounces cellophane noodles

  Salt and white pepper

. . . .

- *Flank Steak*

  ¼ cup peanut oil

  2 teaspoons chopped garlic

  2 teaspoons chopped fresh ginger

  1 pound flank steak, sliced
    into strips

  1½ cups chopped broccoli

  ⅔ cup diced red bell pepper

  1½ cups bean sprouts

  1 cup snow peas

  2 teaspoons rice wine

  ½ cup oyster sauce

  ¼ cup light soy sauce

  1½ teaspoons red pepper flakes

Serves 4

. . . .

*This tasty pork dish is delicious
served with Taro Hash with
Black Beans (page 141).*

SEARED PORK TENDERLOIN WITH A PEANUT AND SESAME CRUST AND PLUM SAUCE

. . . .

- *Crust*

  ½ cup cream-style peanut butter

  ¼ cup coconut milk

  2 teaspoons fish sauce

  ½ teaspoon chopped fresh red
  chili pepper

  4 basil leaves, shredded

  ¼ cup ground roasted peanuts

  Pinch of turmeric

  ¼ cup roasted sesame seeds

. . . .

- *Pork Tenderloin*

  1 (10-ounce) pork tenderloin, cut
  into medallions

  Salt and pepper

  3 teaspoons peanut oil,
  for sautéing

  Serves 2

. . . .

- *Plum Sauce*

  ½ cup dry red wine, preferably
  Cabernet or Pinot Noir

  ½ cup plum wine

  ½ cup rice wine

  ½ cup seeded and quartered ripe
  red plums

  2 cups demi-glace (meat glaze)
  or strong chicken stock
  (page 214) (see Note)

  1 teaspoon chopped fresh ginger

  Salt and pepper to taste

  Makes 1½ cups

. . . .

· In the bowl of a food processor, combine the peanut butter, coconut milk, fish sauce, chili pepper, basil, and peanuts. Work the processor in on-off motions until the ingredients are well combined. Add the turmeric and sesame seeds, and work the processor again until all ingredients are combined. Set this mixture aside.

· Preheat the oven to 350°F.

· Season the pork medallions with salt and pepper. In a nonstick, ovenproof skillet, heat the peanut oil over medium heat and sauté the pork for 1 minute on each side.

· Remove the pan from the heat. Coat the pork medallions with the crust mixture and place the skillet in the oven. Bake for about 10 minutes, then transfer medallions to warmed plates and serve with the Plum Sauce.

- *Plum Sauce*

· In a small saucepan, combine the wines and plums. Bring the liquid to a boil and reduce it by two thirds.

· Transfer the sauce to a blender and puree. Return the sauce to the saucepan and add the demi-glace. Bring to a boil, reduce the heat, and simmer for about 8 minutes.

· Pass the sauce through a fine strainer, pressing firmly to extract all the juices. Add the ginger, season with salt and pepper to taste, and serve.

· Note: If you are using stock, you may need to thicken the sauce with cornstarch. Mix 3 tablespoons of cornstarch with a little cold water. Stir the mixture slowly into the sauce, and bring to a simmer. The sauce should thicken to the point that it will coat the back of a spoon.

If you don't have enough time to make the crepes, use flour tortillas instead.

STIR-FRIED MONGOLIAN FLANK STEAK WITH CHILI-CHIVE CREPES

. . . .

- *Steak*

  2 (8-ounce) flank steaks

  1 cup light soy sauce

  ½ cup rice wine

  ½ cup hoisin sauce

  3 teaspoons minced garlic

  1 teaspoon light brown sugar

  1½ cups water

  1 teaspoon diced fresh red
  chili pepper

. . . .

- *Vegetables*

  ¼ cup peanut oil

  2 teaspoons minced garlic

  1 teaspoon minced fresh ginger

  1 cup bean sprouts

  1 cup Chinese black mushrooms

  1 cup julienned snow peas

  ½ cup shredded carrot

  ½ cup honey

  ¼ cup mustard seeds

. . . .

- *Chili-Chive Crepes*

  6 eggs, beaten

  Dash of salt

  1½ teaspoons chili powder

  1 teaspoon chopped garlic chives

  1 cup all-purpose flour

  1½ cups milk

  Oil or butter, for frying

Serves 4

. . . .

· Remove all visible fat from the steaks. Combine the remaining steak ingredients in a nonreactive dish and mix well. Add the meat and marinate overnight in the refrigerator. When ready to prepare the dish, drain the steaks and cut into ¼-inch strips. Set aside.

· Heat a wok until very hot and add the peanut oil. When the oil is hot, add the flank steak and stir-fry until golden-brown on the outside and medium-rare in the center, about 2 minutes.

· Add the garlic and ginger. Then add the rest of the vegetables, and stir-fry until tender-crisp, about 2 minutes.

· In a small bowl, combine the honey and mustard seeds. Brush the inside of each crepe with the honey-mustard mixture. Place some of the meat-vegetable mixture in the center and roll crepe into a cylinder. Serve at once.

- *Chili-Chive Crepes*

· In a mixing bowl, combine the eggs, salt, chili powder, garlic chives, and flour. Slowly incorporate the milk until you have a smooth batter. Set the batter aside to rest for about 45 minutes.

· Heat a small frying pan and coat it with oil or room-temperature butter. Pour a small amount of batter into the center of the skillet; with a rotating movement, turn the pan until the batter is spread evenly over the bottom.

· Over low heat, cook the crepe until the bottom is golden, about half a minute. With a spatula, turn the crepe and cook the other side until it is golden, another half minute. Remove the crepe from the pan and set it on a piece of wax paper. Continue cooking the crepes, placing them between pieces of wax paper so they won't stick together, until you have 12.

- Preheat oven to 300°F.
- In a shallow pan, season the lamb with the cayenne pepper, paprika, salt, and pepper and marinate until you are ready to cook it, for at least 15 minutes.
- In a saucepan over medium heat, sauté the shallots, mushrooms, and thyme in the olive oil until light brown, 1 or 2 minutes. Add the wine and stir to blend in particles on bottom of pan. Cook rapidly until the liquid is nearly gone. Add the veal stock, bring to a boil, and reduce by two thirds. Strain the mixture and return to the saucepan. Bring it back to a boil and whisk in the butter. Keep warm.
- In a medium ovenproof skillet, sauté the lamb in the peanut oil for 3 minutes on each side. Remove the lamb and set aside. In the same skillet, sauté the garlic over medium heat until light brown, about 30 seconds. Drain the garlic, add to the sauce, and let steep for 5 minutes. Serve with the lamb.

The high quality of game and meat from Molokai is well known throughout the Islands. The livestock is raised without chemical-based food and is allowed to run free, so the meat is as good as it can be.

MOLOKAI LAMB LOIN WITH CABERNET-GARLIC SAUCE

2 (8-ounce) lamb loins
Dash of cayenne pepper
Pinch of paprika
3 teaspoons salt
2 teaspoons pepper
4 shallots, chopped
4 button mushrooms, sliced
1 sprig fresh thyme
2 teaspoons olive oil
1 cup Cabernet or other dry
   red wine
1 cup veal stock
2 teaspoons unsalted butter
1/4 cup peanut oil
15 garlic cloves, chopped

Serves 4

- Prepare the grill.
- Season the inside of the chicken with salt and pepper. Place the thyme and garlic under the skin on the breast.
- Combine the honey, soy sauce, lime juice, and brown sugar; stir until the brown sugar is thoroughly dissolved.
- Place the chicken on the spit and brush with the glaze every few minutes until the glaze starts to stick to the chicken. Continue to roast until chicken is done, about 1½ hours. Remove the chicken from the spit and let rest for 10 minutes before carving.

"Huli-huli" is the ancient Hawaiian method of roasting on a spit. If a spit is not available, just roast the chicken in your oven on a rack with a cup of water in the roasting pan. The chicken juices, the marinade, and the water will mix to make a wonderful glaze to baste the chicken with. Brushed every 5 minutes or so with this glaze, the chicken becomes golden brown on the outside while retaining all its flavors and juices inside. Inserting the thyme and garlic beneath the skin adds extra flavor.

HULI-HULI ROASTED CHICKEN WITH LIME-HONEY GLAZE

. . . .

1 (2- to 3-pound) free-range
   chicken
Salt and pepper
4 sprigs fresh thyme
2 garlic cloves, sliced thin
1 cup honey
1 cup dark soy sauce
1 cup lime juice
3 teaspoons light brown sugar

Serves 4

. . . .

Many flavors are discernible in this dish, especially the pungent tastes of peanut and garlic. This is a good example of how versatile and well balanced the flavors are in Asian cooking.

STIR-FRIED ISLAND CHICKEN WITH PEANUT-GARLIC SAUCE

. . . .

- *Peanut-Garlic Sauce*

  2 teaspoons cream-style
    peanut butter
  2 tablespoons fish sauce
  2 tablespoons chicken stock
    (page 214)
  1 teaspoon minced garlic
  1 teaspoon red curry paste
    (page 216)

. . . .

- *Chicken*

  3 tablespoons peanut oil
  3 teaspoons minced garlic
  1½ teaspoons minced fresh ginger
  9 ounces diced boneless chicken
  1 cup chopped carrots
  1 cup chopped zucchini
  1 cup chopped yellow
    summer squash
  1 cup bean sprouts
  8 teaspoons chopped
    roasted peanuts
  3 tablespoons chicken stock
    (page 214; optional)
  4 teaspoons chopped fresh
    coriander, for garnish

Serves 4

. . . .

· Put the peanut butter in a blender and add the fish sauce and stock. Blend well. Add the garlic and curry paste and blend until smooth.

· In a wok, heat the peanut oil until very hot. Add the garlic and ginger and stir for just a few seconds. Add the chicken. When cooked halfway, add the carrots and stir for a minute or two. Continue adding the vegetables, stirring for a minute after each one. Stir-fry for 1 to 2 minutes.

· Add the peanuts and sauce and mix well. If the sauce is too thick, add the stock. To serve, sprinkle coriander on each portion.

Wild turkeys are found on Molokai and Lanai, but this recipe is just as good if you use a domestic turkey. Mountain apples, which taste something like an apple, are small red fruits that grow in Hawaii. If you can't find them, substitute regular apples. You can prepare this recipe on a spit as well as in your oven. The oven preparation is given here.

Huli-Huli Wild Turkey with Mountain-Apple Dressing

· Preheat the oven to 350°F.

· In a large mixing bowl, combine the bread crumbs, garlic, onions, ginger, sage, carrot, apples, salt and pepper, milk, and eggs. Mix with a spatula until well combined.

· Season the turkey on the outside with coarse salt and cracked pepper. Stuff the turkey's cavity and truss. Place in roasting pan and roast for 5½ to 6 hours, basting frequently with the pan drippings. Let turkey rest for 15 minutes before carving.

. . . .

3 cups bread crumbs

2 teaspoons chopped garlic

2 Maui onions, chopped

2 teaspoons minced fresh ginger

6 sage leaves, minced

1 medium carrot, chopped

5 mountain apples, cored
   and cubed

Salt and pepper

1 cup milk

4 eggs, lightly beaten

1 (20-pound) turkey

Coarse salt

Cracked fresh peppercorns

Serves 8–10

. . . .

The marinade for this rack of lamb caramelizes as it cooks, keeping the meat very tender.

Hunan Rack of Lamb with Five-Spice Sauce

. . . .

- *Meat*

  3 cups oyster sauce

  ½ cup whiskey

  2 garlic cloves, crushed

  2 teaspoons chopped fresh
  chili pepper

  2 cups dark soy sauce

  1 cup hoisin sauce

  3 cups water

  2 teaspoons sugar

  2 racks of lamb, about 3 pounds
  total, fat removed

. . . .

- *Sauce*

  2 cups dry red wine, such as
  Cabernet Sauvignon

  2 teaspoons minced garlic

  2 star anise

  ¼ cup hoisin sauce

  2 teaspoons minced fresh ginger

  2 cups demi-glace (meat glaze)
  or strong chicken stock
  (page 214)

  1 teaspoon five-spice powder

  Serves 4

. . . .

· Combine oyster sauce, whiskey, garlic, chili pepper, soy sauce, hoisin sauce, water, and sugar, and marinate the lamb for 12 hours in the refrigerator.

· Prepare the grill. Drain the meat and discard the marinade. Grill slowly for 8 to 10 minutes, or until medium-rare, turning the rack frequently. Because of the sugar in the marinade, the lamb will color rapidly, so avoid cooking too quickly. Remove from grill and keep warm.

· In a nonreactive saucepan, combine the wine, garlic, star anise, hoisin sauce, and ginger. Over high heat, reduce by two thirds, then add the demi-glace. Add the five-spice powder and simmer for 15 minutes more.

· Slice lamb into chops and divide among 4 serving plates. Pour the sauce over lamb and serve.

Meat and Poultry

Maui onions are on the sweet side, and when cooked to a crisp they taste almost like candy. You can cut them into ¼-inch slices or into paper-thin slices, which will cook more quickly and be crisper. The paniolos are the cowboys of Hawaii, and this is by all means a rustic and hearty recipe. If you grill the steak you can use kiawe wood or charcoal to bring even more flavor to this dish.

GRILLED PANIOLO STEAK WITH MAUI ONION RINGS

1 cup dark soy sauce

¼ cup dry sherry

6 tablespoons minced fresh
    ginger

6 garlic cloves, minced

4 (9-ounce) T-bone steaks

Oil for deep-frying

4 Maui onions

1 cup milk

1 cup all-purpose flour

Salt and pepper

Serves 4–6

· In a shallow pan, combine the soy sauce, sherry, ginger, garlic, and steaks and marinate for about 2 hours.

· Prepare the grill.

· Heat the oil to 375°F in a large saucepan. Peel and slice the Maui onions thinly. Dip the slices into the milk and immediately into the flour. Shake off the excess flour, and deep-fry in hot oil until crisp and golden, about 2 minutes. Season with salt and pepper and keep warm.

· Remove the steaks from the marinade. Grill the steaks over high heat for 3 to 5 minutes on each side. Serve with the onion rings.

Hana is a small, remote village at the eastern end of the island of Maui, where the old ways are still very much alive. To drive there is to experience natural Hawaii at its best—waterfalls, flowers, birds, and blue waters. The inhabitants still fish using traditional throwing nets and hunt wild pigs in the mountains. • If you can't find T-bone pork chops, this preparation is excellent with rib or loin pork chops or pork tenderloin, and it is great served with Taro Hash (page 141) and Grilled Corn and Maui Onion Relish (page 189).

HANA-STYLE GRILLED T-BONE PORK CHOPS

· In a large, shallow, nonreactive bowl, combine the soy sauce, garlic, oyster sauce, red pepper flakes, and scallions. Add the chops and marinate, refrigerated, for at least 3 hours.
· Prepare the grill.
· Drain the chops and grill for 10 to 12 minutes, depending on thickness, until thoroughly cooked but not dried out.

. . . .

2 cups light soy sauce
3 garlic cloves, crushed
1 cup oyster sauce
1 teaspoon red pepper flakes
2 scallions, chopped
4 (12-ounce) T-bone pork chops

Serves 4

. . . .

Tamarind is the tart fruit of the tamarind tree—a dark, sticky pod that is used to season curries, stews, and soups. It is native to India, but has become essential to Indonesian cooking. You can find fresh pods and seedless pulp in packages in Asian stores.

KAMADO-SMOKED PORK CHOPS WITH TAMARIND PLUM SAUCE

- Brush each pork chop with olive oil, season with salt and coarsely ground black pepper, and set aside.
- Build a fire in a kamado (Japanese smoker) using the guava chips. When the fire is hot, place the pork chops in the smoker and smoke for approximately 7 minutes per side. Serve with Tamarind Plum Sauce.

- *Tamarind Plum Sauce*
- Combine the wine, plums, and tamarind in a saucepan, bring to a boil, and reduce the heat. Cook until the mixture is reduced by two thirds.
- Add the chicken stock and bring to a boil. Reduce the heat and simmer for about 5 minutes. Whisk in the cornstarch mixture and cook for another 5 minutes. Strain the sauce and season with salt and pepper to taste.

. . . .

4 (8-ounce) pork chops
¼ cup olive oil
Salt and freshly ground black pepper
1 cup guava wood chips

Serves 4

. . . .

- *Tamarind Plum Sauce*
2 cups dry red wine
4 ripe plums, pitted
1 ounce seedless tamarind pulp
1 quart chicken stock
4 teaspoons cornstarch mixed with ⅓ cup cold water
Salt and pepper

Makes 1½ cups

. . . .

Steaming is an unusual way of cooking lamb, but in this recipe the flavors of lamb and ginger— sealed by the rice paper—combine to form a rich taste and aroma that make you forget that there is no fat involved with the cooking, which makes this a great recipe for those who love lamb but are watching their fat intake.

Steamed Australian Lamb Loin with Tamarind Plum Sauce

. . . .

1 large zucchini squash
2 yellow summer squash
4 leeks, white part only
4-inch piece fresh ginger
4 (8-ounce) lamb loin slices
Salt and freshly ground pepper
Cayenne pepper
4 sheets rice paper
8 leaves bok choy
Tamarind Plum Sauce (page 131)

Serves 4

. . . .

· Julienne the squash and leeks as finely as possible. Peel the ginger and cut into four 1-inch chunks. Julienne each piece as finely as possible. Set the vegetables aside.

· Season the lamb with the salt, pepper, and cayenne. Set aside.

· Moisten each sheet of rice paper and line it with 2 bok choy leaves. Place a quarter of the vegetable mixture on each wrapper and add a lamb slice. Wrap the meat tightly in the bok choy leaves and rice paper. Gently place the lamb packages in a bamboo steamer, cover, and steam over boiling water for about 6 minutes, at which point is should be medium-rare. Allow to rest for one minute.

· Cut the lamb packages into 1½-inch slices. Place some Tamarind Plum Sauce on a serving plate, place one sliced package on top of the sauce, and serve.

*The peanut and sesame crust
brings out the flavors of the lamb
and keeps the rack very moist.*

· Trim the lamb of visible fat. Season with cumin, salt, and
ginger and let stand for 1 hour.
· Preheat the oven to 375°F.
· In a medium mixing bowl, combine the bread crumbs,
sesame seeds, peanut butter, and butter. Mix until the consistency of a paste.
· Coat the top of the racks with the paste to about ½-inch
thick. Cook for about 10 minutes, until medium-rare. Allow
rack to rest for a few minutes in a warm place, then cut into
chops. Serve with Plum Sauce.

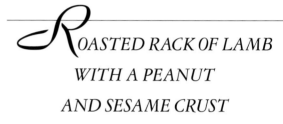

ROASTED RACK OF LAMB WITH A PEANUT AND SESAME CRUST

. . . .

2 racks of lamb, about
   3 pounds total
2 teaspoons ground cumin
2 teaspoons salt
1 teaspoon ground ginger
1 cup bread crumbs
¼ cup toasted sesame seeds
¼ cup cream-style peanut butter
½ cup (1 stick) unsalted
   butter, softened
Plum Sauce (page 118)

Serves 4

. . . .

This hearty, unsophisticated dish is very satisfying. Sometimes your stomach wants a simple stew, and this one delivers good, strong flavors. In Hawaii, people add some roasted nuts as a garnish just before serving.

Country-Style Beef Stew

....

1½ pounds bottom round of beef

Salt and pepper

3 garlic cloves, crushed

¼ cup vegetable oil

½ cup all-purpose flour

2 tablespoons tomato paste

1 cup chicken stock (page 214)

1 cup water

1½ cups diced carrots

1 cup sliced string beans

½ cup chopped celery

1 cup diced turnip

3 large tomatoes, diced

1 bay leaf

¼ cup thinly sliced fresh ginger

2 teaspoons fish sauce

Serves 4–6

....

· Cut the beef into 2-inch pieces and season with salt and pepper. Rub pieces on all sides with the crushed garlic.

· In a large soup pot, heat the oil over medium heat. When the oil is hot, brown the meat until well colored, then add the flour and sauté for a few minutes more. Add the tomato paste and cook for 1 minute. Add the stock and water, mix gently with the meat, and bring to a boil. Add the carrots, beans, celery, turnip, tomatoes, bay leaf, ginger, and fish sauce. Return to a boil, lower the heat, and simmer for about 1½ hours.

· Serve over steamed rice.

- In a saucepan, combine the bay leaf, garlic, vinegar, salt, pork, chicken, and water. Stir well and bring to a boil. Simmer until the meat is tender, about 15 to 20 minutes, adding water if needed to keep mixture moist. Drain the meat and reserve the cooking juices.
- Using a hand-held strainer, remove the garlic from the liquid. In a skillet, heat the olive oil and when it is hot, add the garlic. Sauté until the garlic turns golden, then add the chicken and pork and sauté until the meat is golden or lightly browned. Add the reserved cooking stock to the pan, followed by the lobster. Simmer for about 5 minutes, then add the soy sauce, tomatoes, and coriander. Cook for another minute or so, and serve at once.

Adobo is widely considered to be the national dish of the Philippines. The flavors balance beautifully in this dish, especially with the sour tang of the vinegar. The lobster in this dish is my own variation, but you can also make it with shrimp—or simply with chicken and pork.

CHICKEN, PORK, AND LOBSTER ADOBO

. . . .

1 bay leaf

4 garlic cloves, flattened with the flat side of a knife and peeled

½ cup white wine vinegar

Pinch of coarse salt

½ pound boneless pork butt, cut into small pieces

1½ pounds skinless, boneless chicken breasts, cut into cubes

½ cup water

4 teaspoons olive oil

8 ounces cooked lobster, cut into pieces

3 tablespoons light soy sauce

2 medium tomatoes, cut into cubes

3 teaspoons fresh coriander

Serves 4–6

. . . .

5

Vegetables and Side Dishes

This recipe can also be made with snow peas or green beans, but stir-fry them quickly to keep them crisp!

STIR-FRIED SUGAR SNAP PEAS WITH GINGER AND BLACK BEANS

2 teaspoons peanut oil

1 teaspoon minced fresh ginger

1 teaspoon minced garlic

2 cups sugar snap peas

2 teaspoons chopped fermented
    black beans

1 teaspoon fish sauce

3 basil leaves, shredded

Serves 4

· Heat a wok, then add the peanut oil along with the ginger and garlic and fry until lightly golden. Add the sugar snap peas and stir-fry for a few seconds only, so they remain crispy. Add the black beans, fish sauce, and basil. Stir well and serve immediately.

At my restaurant, we use only
pencil-thin asparagus grown by
Alice Hoshide on Kauai, which
is tender and doesn't need to
be peeled. But you can use any
asparagus for this dish. It can
be served as a main course or as
an accompaniment to swordfish
or marlin. The combination of
asparagus, sesame seeds, and pine
nuts is unbelievable.

STIR-FRIED ASPARAGUS WITH SESAME SEEDS AND PINE NUTS

· Place the sesame oil in a wok and heat until the oil is very hot. Add the ginger and stir for a few seconds. Add the asparagus and stir-fry for a couple of minutes, until it is cooked but still firm and bright green. Add the red pepper, scallions, pine nuts, and sesame seeds, and mix well. Season with salt and pepper to taste and serve at once.

. . . .

3 teaspoons roasted sesame oil
3 teaspoons minced fresh ginger
12 thick asparagus stalks,
   peeled and washed
¼ cup julienned red bell pepper
¼ cup julienned scallions
¼ cup toasted pine nuts
1½ teaspoons toasted white
   sesame seeds
Salt and pepper

Serves 4

. . . .

· In a wok set over high heat, combine the peanut and sesame oils. When they are hot, add the ginger and garlic and stir for a few seconds. Add the taro and stir-fry until the taro is golden. Add the zucchini, snow peas, and carrots and stir-fry until the vegetables are cooked but still crispy.

· Add the fermented black beans and mix well. Garnish with the chopped sage and fresh coriander and serve at once.

Taro, a highly nutritious tuber that reminds those who eat it of potatoes and chestnuts, is an important staple in the Pacific Islands. In the old days it was mostly used to make poi, but we've been working on new ways to use taro—as hash, French fries, and chips—with Javellana Farms on Kauai. Two types of taro are cultivated in Hawaii. One, grown in flooded fields, is used to make poi. The other, used in other dishes, grows in dry fields.

TARO HASH
WITH BLACK BEANS

. . . .

2 teaspoons peanut oil
½ teaspoon roasted sesame oil
½ teaspoon minced fresh ginger
½ teaspoon minced garlic
2⅔ cups shredded taro
¼ cup sliced zucchini
¼ cup sliced snow peas
¼ cup sliced carrot
2 teaspoons chopped fermented
    black beans
1 teaspoon chopped fresh sage
½ teaspoon chopped fresh
    coriander

Serves 4

. . . .

I love risotto because the rice itself is very flavorful and it can be flavored so deliciously, in this case with the unorthodox combination—for risotto—of kaffir lime leaves, ginger, and scallions. It is a great accompaniment to fish.

ORIENTAL RISOTTO WITH CHILI PEPPERS AND SCALLIONS

. . . .

2 tablespoons olive oil

2 tablespoons sesame oil

2 teaspoon chopped garlic

2 teaspoons chopped fresh ginger

½ medium onion, chopped

8 ounces Arborio rice

½ cup dry white wine

2½ cups clam juice or chicken
     stock (page 214)

3 tablespoons reduced-sodium
     soy sauce

2 tablespoons chopped fresh
     coriander

¼ cup sliced scallions

2 tablespoons julienned kaffir
     lime leaf

1 teaspoon chopped red
     chili pepper

Serves 4

. . . .

· Heat the clam juice or stock to a slow boil in a small saucepan.

· In a large saucepan, heat the olive and sesame oils over medium heat. Add the garlic, ginger, and onion and sauté gently for about 2 minutes, until they become soft. Add the rice and stir thoroughly for about 1 minute. Add the wine, reduce the heat to low, and stir continuously. When the liquid is almost completely gone, add 1 cup of hot clam juice. Keep stirring, and when the liquid is nearly gone add another ½ cup of clam juice. Repeat until the rice is cooked, about 13 minutes. Add the soy sauce, fresh coriander, scallion, kaffir lime leaf, and chili pepper and mix thoroughly. Serve immediately.

· Combine the Parmesan, ginger, coriander, scallions, lime juice, and olive oil in a mixing bowl. Season to taste with salt and pepper. Reserve in the refrigerator until ready to use.

· In a large skillet, heat 2 tablespoons olive oil over high heat. Add the mushrooms, zucchini, carrots, peppers, snow peas, and red pepper flakes and stir-fry until crisp. Put aside in a warm place until ready to use.

· Bring a large pot of water to a boil. Add salt and 1 tablespoon olive oil. Cook the pasta for about 2 minutes, or until it is cooked but firm. Drain the pasta well and add the reserved vegetables and the pesto. Mix well and season with salt and pepper to taste. Serve immediately.

This light and flavorful pasta can be served as a side dish with shrimp or chicken. I like to keep the vegetables on the chunky side so you can distinguish the different tastes.

ASIAN LINGUINE WITH SHIITAKE MUSHROOM AND CHINESE PESTO

- *Pesto*

    4 teaspoons grated Parmesan cheese
    4 teaspoons chopped fresh ginger
    ⅓ cup chopped fresh coriander
    1 tablespoon minced garlic
    4 scallions, sliced
    Juice of one lime
    ⅓ cup olive oil
    Salt and pepper

- *Pasta*

    3 tablespoons olive oil
    2 cups sliced Shiitake mushrooms
    1 cup julienned zucchini
    1 cup julienned carrots
    ½ cup julienned red bell pepper
    1 cup snow peas
    ½ teaspoon red pepper flakes
    1 pound fresh linguine
    Salt and pepper

    Serves 4

· Heat the peanut oil in a wok. When the oil starts to smoke, add the bacon and cook until light brown. Add the garlic and mushrooms, starting with the shiitake, then the black mushrooms, golden mushrooms, and the enoki. Stir-fry each for about 2 minutes before adding next. Finish by adding the coriander.

This dish can be served as an appetizer or as a vegetable accompaniment. It makes a wonderful garnish for lamb or pork, or you can add a little balsamic vinegar and serve with any snapper instead of a sauce. Cut the mushrooms into big pieces, since they will shrink a little when stir-fried.

STIR-FRIED WILD MUSHROOMS WITH BACON, GARLIC, AND CORIANDER

. . . .

2 teaspoons peanut oil

5 ounces bacon, chopped into
    1-inch pieces

2 teaspoons chopped garlic

4 ounces medium shiitake
    mushrooms

4 ounces Chinese black
    mushrooms

4 ounces golden mushrooms

4 ounces enoki mushrooms

1 tablespoon chopped fresh
    coriander

Serves 4

. . . .

*The flavor of freshly grilled egg-
plant with spicy goat cheese and
fresh basil is close to perfect. I get
fresh goat cheese from Ku'oko'a
Farm on the Big Island. They
also produce a macadamia chèvre
that is great with eggplant.*

GRILLED JAPANESE EGGPLANT WITH GARLIC-CHILI GOAT CHEESE

· Prepare the grill.

· Cut the eggplants in half lengthwise. Brush the cut edges with olive oil and season with salt and pepper.

· In a mixing bowl combine the cheese, garlic, red pepper flakes, basil, and a pinch of salt, and blend well. Refrigerate until ready to use.

· Place the eggplant halves on the grill flesh side down and cook until almost soft, about 2 minutes. Remove from the grill and let cool slightly.

· Spread the goat cheese mixture on the warm eggplant pieces and serve at once.

. . . .

8 Japanese eggplants

Olive oil

Salt and pepper

½ pound fresh mild goat
    cheese (chèvre)

2 teaspoons minced garlic

1 teaspoon red pepper flakes

6 basil leaves, shredded

Serves 4

. . . .

Eggplant lovers beware: this dish can be addictive. The spicy chili oil really brings out the eggplant flavor. It goes well with lamb or a whole fish.

STIR-FRIED EGGPLANT WITH CHILI OIL, GARLIC, AND BASIL

. . . .

⅓ cup chili oil

3 medium Japanese eggplants,
    cut into 2-inch matchstick
    julienne

3 teaspoons minced garlic

1 teaspoon minced fresh ginger

¼ cup dry sherry

2 teaspoons oyster sauce

½ teaspoon coriander seeds

14 small basil leaves

Juice of 1 lemon

4 scallions, thinly sliced

Serves 4

. . . .

· Heat a wok until hot and add the chili oil. When the oil is hot, add the eggplant and stir-fry until the pieces are crisp and golden. Add the garlic and ginger, and stir-fry again for a few seconds. Add the sherry and oyster sauce. Reduce for just 1 minute, then add the coriander, basil, lemon juice, and scallions. Mix well and serve at once.

- Preheat oven to 325°F.
- Place the olive oil in a small ovenproof skillet. Add the garlic and bake for 20 minutes. Remove from the oven and drain the garlic from the olive oil. Chop garlic as finely as possible, until it is pureed, and reserve.
- Heat the cream in a small saucepan until it reaches the boil.
- At the same time, set a vegetable steamer over boiling water. Peel the potatoes and cut into quarters. Steam them for about 15 to 20 minutes, until they break slightly when pressed with a finger. Put potatoes through a food mill and season to taste with salt and white pepper. Add five-spice powder and reserved garlic and mix thoroughly. Mix in butter and slowly incorporate the hot cream, mixing continuously until the potatoes become smooth and light. Serve immediately.

In the 1980s, many restaurants turned their backs on the simple garnishes to indulge in baby vegetables, which do not require so much preparation. But these days, people are returning to comforting old standards, such as mashed potatoes. I remember how much I enjoyed my grandmother's classic mashed potatoes when I was a child, but in this recipe I've given them a Pacific twist. They are good with practically anything.

MASHED POTATOES WITH ROASTED GARLIC AND FIVE-SPICE POWDER

. . . .

3 tablespoons olive oil
3 garlic cloves, peeled
½ cup heavy cream
4 medium white potatoes
Salt and white pepper
3 pinches five-spice powder
½ cup (1 stick) unsalted
    butter, softened

Serves 4

. . . .

This tasty puree has nothing to do with expensive sturgeon eggs, but when eggplant is roasted and chopped it does resemble caviar. This dish has deep roots in the south of France, and it is delicious with grilled sourdough bread. • Deep-fried lotus root is a welcome change from the familiar potato chip. You can use the same method to make chips from many different vegetables, such as sweet potatoes and taro root.

$\mathcal{E}$GGPLANT CAVIAR WITH DEEP-FRIED LOTUS ROOT

. . . .

- *Eggplant Caviar*
  2 medium eggplant
  Salt and pepper
  ¼ cup extra virgin olive oil
  2 teaspoons minced garlic
  8 large basil leaves, julienned
. . . .
- *Deep-Fried Lotus Root*
  1 medium lotus root
  Oil for deep-frying
  Salt and white pepper

  Serves 4
. . . .

- *Eggplant Caviar*
  · Preheat oven to 375°F.
  · Split the eggplants through the middle. With the tip of a paring knife, score the cut flesh to a depth of 2 inches. Place cut side up on an oiled baking sheet or ovenproof skillet. Season with salt and pepper and pour the olive oil evenly over the tops. Bake for about 20 minutes, until the eggplants are completely soft inside and the top is crispy. Remove from the oven and set aside to cool completely.
  · When cool, scoop out the insides. Mix in the garlic and basil and place on a large chopping board. Chop the mixture with a chef's knife until it is almost a paste, but with some texture remaining. Taste for seasoning and serve hot or cold with Deep-Fried Lotus Root.
  · Note: Eggplant Caviar will keep in the refrigerator for several days.

- *Deep-Fried Lotus Root*
  · Peel and slice the lotus root into ¼-inch slices. Heat oil in deep saucepan to 375°F, and deep-fry lotus until crisp and golden, about 2 minutes. Season with salt and pepper, and reserve.

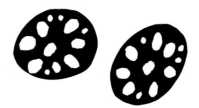

Stir-fried rice is a great way to use leftover rice, and this version is a good accompaniment to both fish and meat dishes. Although the recipe calls for Portuguese sausage, you can use any kind of sausage you like, depending on the taste you want to achieve. I have had good results using Cajun sausage and garlic sausage.

STIR-FRIED RICE WITH PORTUGUESE SAUSAGE

. . . .

2 tablespoons roasted sesame oil
2 cups diced cooked Portuguese
    sausage (linguica)
2 teaspoons chopped fresh ginger
3 garlic cloves, minced
¼ cup diced carrot
¼ cup diced celery
¼ cup diced onion
3 cups cooked white rice
2 eggs
1 tablespoon oyster sauce
2 teaspoons light soy sauce
Pepper (see Note)
¼ cup diced scallions

Serves 4

. . . .

· In a wok over high heat, heat the oil and cook the sausage until lightly browned. Add the ginger and garlic and cook for a few seconds more. Add vegetables and stir-fry until tender-crisp, about 3 minutes. Add the rice and mix well. Make a well in the center of the rice mixture and add the eggs. Let them cook for 2 minutes, then stir them into the rice mixture. Add the oyster sauce and the soy sauce and mix well. Season with pepper and garnish with scallions, and serve immediately.
· Note: If the sausage you use is very peppery, you may not want to add additional pepper.

- In a sauté pan, gently heat the coconut cream until it just starts to separate. Remove from the heat.
- In a large wok over high heat, heat the olive oil and stir-fry the garlic until golden. Add the curry paste and cook for 1 minute, stirring constantly. Reduce the heat and add the coconut cream and diced potato. Slowly bring the mixture to a boil, stirring often to avoid burning.
- In a large skillet, heat the peanut oil until it is very hot and add the tomatoes, eggplant, zucchini, squash, peppers, and onion. Sauté the vegetables until they are tender, then add them to the coconut mixture in the wok. Season to taste with salt and pepper, add the stock and lemon juice, and cook until the vegetables are soft, about 8 minutes.

This Asian-flavored ratatouille can be served with Kamado-Smoked Peppered Kajiki (page 99) or with any grilled or steamed fish.

GREEN CURRY RATATOUILLE

. . . .

⅓ cup coconut milk

1 cup olive oil

2 garlic cloves, minced

1 teaspoon green curry paste (page 216)

⅔ cup diced peeled potato

⅓ cup peanut oil

2 medium tomatoes, peeled, seeded, and diced

1 cup diced Japanese eggplant

⅔ cup diced zucchini

⅔ cup diced yellow summer squash

⅔ cup diced red bell pepper

⅔ cup diced green bell pepper

½ cup diced onion

Salt and pepper

1 cup chicken stock (page 214) or water

Juice of 1 lemon

Serves 4

. . . .

Many people avoid tofu because of its "flat" taste, but by combining it with taro chips and adding stir-fried vegetables with black beans topped with strong, chunky pesto, you have a dish that is full of flavor. If you want to cut down on deep-fried foods, you can warm the tofu in a 350°F oven for a minute, and then proceed with the recipe.

TOFU TEMPURA WITH TARO LASAGNA, BLACK BEANS, AND GINGER-SCALLION PESTO

Oil for deep-frying
3 teaspoons olive oil
1 teaspoon minced garlic
1 teaspoon minced fresh ginger
⅓ cup julienned carrots
⅓ cup julienned zucchini
⅓ cup julienned snow peas
⅓ cup small broccoli florets
¼ cup bean sprouts
3 teaspoons light soy sauce
2 teaspoons finely chopped
   fermented black beans
8 (¼-inch-thick) slices taro
   or potato
Salt
5 ounces extra-firm tofu, sliced
2 cups tempura batter (page 85)
Ground black pepper
4 teaspoons Ginger-Scallion
   Pesto (page 186)

Serves 4

· Heat the oil in a deep-fryer to about 375°F.
· Put olive oil in a wok and add the garlic and ginger. Fry just until golden.
· Add the carrots, zucchini, snow peas, broccoli, and bean sprouts; stir-fry lightly so vegetables are on the crispy side. Add the soy sauce and fermented black beans. Mix well, remove from heat, and set aside.
· Deep-fry the potato or taro chips until golden crisp. Season with salt. Set aside.
· Dip the tofu slices into the tempura batter and cook until golden; drain on a paper towel and season with black pepper.
· Layer the "lasagna" in a 10-inch dish, starting with a layer of the deep-fried taro or potato chips, then the sautéed vegetables, then the pesto. Repeat until all the ingredients are used.

The soil on Kauai is especially rich and almost anything can be grown there, so I serve organic produce from local farmers at my restaurant. Gary Gunderson produces some of the best broccoli in the vicinity. It's so tender that the stems can be served along with the florets.

STEAMED BROCCOLI WITH SESAME SEEDS, TOFU, AND OYSTER SAUCE

. . . .

2 medium stalks broccoli,
   stems removed
½ cup diced extra-firm tofu
¼ cup oyster sauce
½ teaspoon minced garlic
½ teaspoon minced fresh
   chili pepper
2 teaspoons pickled red ginger
½ teaspoon red miso
¼ cup rice wine
3 teaspoons toasted white
   sesame seeds

Serves 4

. . . .

· Cut the broccoli into florets and, along with the diced tofu, place in a steamer set inside a medium saucepan over boiling water. Steam for about 2 minutes. The broccoli should stay bright green and on the firm side.

· In a wok over high heat, combine the oyster sauce, garlic, chili pepper, ginger, miso, and rice wine. Bring to a boil. Add the broccoli and tofu and mix well. Garnish with the sesame seeds and serve at once.

When I first arrived on Kauai, five years ago, it was very difficult to purchase what I needed for the restaurant on the island. Most of my produce came from abroad. That situation has changed and I feel blessed that some of the best farmers I have ever met are now supplying me with fresh vegetables. Kauai has very rich soil and the fruits and vegetables grown here have a lot of flavor. This recipe uses thai soi, a member of the cabbage family, which has beautiful green leaves and a light, bitter taste. It can be served by itself or as a garnish for meat or poultry.

· Split each head of thai soi in half and wash thoroughly under cold running water. Drain on paper towels until dry.
· In a large skillet, heat the oil over high heat and sauté the thai soi for about 2 minutes on each side. Remove to a serving platter and keep warm.
· Add the walnuts to the skillet and cook, stirring constantly, for about 2 minutes. Add the honey and reduce the heat to medium. Cook until the honey turns a caramel color, about 2 minutes. Pour the nut mixture over the thai soi, garnish with sesame seeds, and serve immediately.

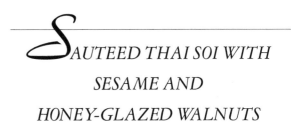

SAUTEED THAI SOI WITH SESAME AND HONEY-GLAZED WALNUTS

. . . .

2 heads thai soi
¼ cup peanut oil
1 cup walnut halves
1 cup honey
4 teaspoons toasted white
   sesame seeds

Serves 4

. . . .

Macadamia and Pineapple

Rice Pilaf and Stir-Fried

Rice with Portuguese Sausage

Rice is the staple food of Hawaii, and my good friend Sam Choy always finds delicious new ways to serve it. This pilaf goes well with roast pork and with shrimp.

Macadamia and Pineapple Rice Pilaf

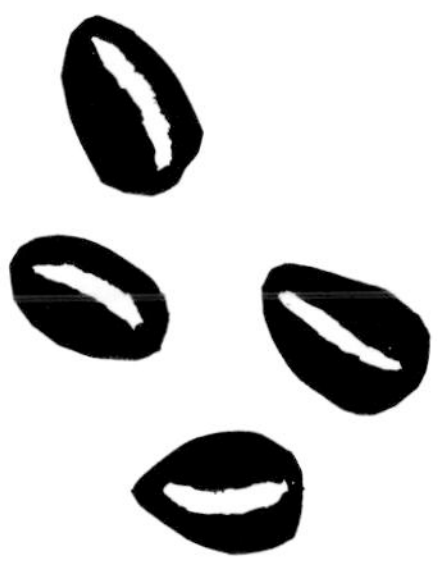

1 tablespoon unsalted butter
1½ cups long-grain white rice
2 teaspoons minced garlic
¼ cup diced red bell pepper
¼ cup diced yellow bell pepper
3 cups strong chicken stock (page 214)
½ cup golden raisins
½ cup chopped roasted macadamia nuts, preferably unsalted
1 sage leaf
½ teaspoon salt
⅓ cup chopped fresh coriander
1 cup diced pineapple

Serves 4

- Preheat the oven to 375°F.
- In a flameproof casserole, melt the butter and add the rice. Stir for a few seconds, until the butter coats the rice. Add the garlic and stir for a few seconds, but not long enough to let the rice change color. Add the red and yellow peppers and cook for a few seconds, again not long enough to let the peppers change color. Add the stock and bring the mixture gently to a boil. Add the raisins, nuts, sage, and salt. Cover, place in oven, and bake for about 18 minutes.
- Remove the dish from the oven and let rest for about 10 minutes. Add the coriander and pineapple. Season if necessary and serve at once.
- Note: If you use salted macadamia nuts, you won't have to add the salt.

When I was in boarding school, Thursday was Lentil Day. For years after I avoided cooking with lentils, until my interest in nutrition made me rediscover them. Green curry and basil combined with lentils makes a deliciously uncommon and interesting combination, a far cry from the lentils of my youth.

GREEN AND YELLOW LENTILS WITH GREEN CURRY BASIL

. . . .

2 cups uncooked green lentils

2 cups uncooked yellow lentils

2 teaspoons unsalted butter

2 teaspoons minced garlic

1 medium onion, chopped

1 cup dry white wine

2 cups chicken stock (page 214)

1 cup coconut milk

2 teaspoons green curry paste
  (page 216)

4 kaffir lime leaves, shredded

6 leaves fresh basil, shredded

Serves 4

. . . .

· Soak the lentils in cold water for about 2 hours before cooking. Drain and set aside until ready to use.

· In a large saucepan, melt the butter over medium heat. Add the garlic and onion and sauté for about 3 minutes, stirring frequently. Add the lentils and stir well, then add the wine and reduce by two thirds. Add the stock and bring to a boil, cooking gently for about 10 minutes. Stir in the coconut milk and green curry paste, and add the kaffir lime leaves and basil.

· Serve hot as a vegetable side dish or as a garnish with a chicken dish.

- *Filling*
  - In a nonreactive skillet, heat ¼ cup olive oil over medium heat. Add the shallots, garlic, fennel, and artichoke and sauté slowly for about 2 minutes, taking care that they do not color. Add the wine and reduce until the liquid is almost completely gone. Add ¼ cup chicken stock and let reduce for 3 minutes. Add the bok choy, stir completely, and let simmer for another 2 minutes. Add the vinegar, sage, and thyme and reserve until completely cool.

- *Crust*
  - Make the crust mixture. Combine the bread crumbs, Parmesan, nutmeg, garlic, and butter and season with salt and pepper. Reserve at room temperature.
  - Preheat oven to 350°F. Bring a large pan of water to the boil and add salt and the olive oil. Take a baking sheet and brush with the remaining oil. Place the pasta sheets, 2 at a time, in the boiling water and cook for about 30 seconds. Remove from water, drain, and place flat on the baking sheet. Repeat until all sheets are cooked. Season the pasta with salt and pepper and sprinkle Parmesan over them. Place ⅛ of the filling in the center of each sheet and roll into an even cylinder. Place the cannelloni, seam-side down, in a deep baking dish and pour in the remaining stock. Scatter the reserved crust mixture over the top and bake for about 10 minutes, until crust in golden brown. Serve immediately.

The taste of fresh fennel is especially good when combined with artichoke. These cannelloni are baked with a little chicken broth and sherry vinegar, and have a delicious crust on top.

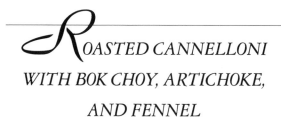

ROASTED CANNELLONI WITH BOK CHOY, ARTICHOKE, AND FENNEL

- *Filling*
  ½ cup olive oil
  2 shallots, minced
  1 teaspoon minced garlic
  ½ fennel bulb, diced small
  3 artichoke hearts, diced small
  ½ cup dry white wine
  ¾ cup chicken stock (page 214)
  2 cups bok choy
  1 tablespoon sherry vinegar
  2 teaspoons chopped fresh sage
  2 teaspoons chopped fresh thyme

- *Crust*
  ½ cup bread crumbs
  ½ cup Parmesan cheese
  1 pinch freshly ground nutmeg
  1 tablespoon minced garlic
  4 tablespoons butter, softened
  Salt and pepper

  1 tablespoon olive oil
  8 3-inch square pasta sheets
     (page 215)
  4 tablespoons freshly grated
     Parmesan cheese
  Salt and pepper

  Serves 4

6

Sauces and Relishes

*I love the nutty taste of black
sesame seeds. If you can't find
them, use toasted white sesame
seeds instead. This dressing may
thicken a bit when made in a
blender, but it will still coat
a salad well.*

BLACK SESAME DRESSING

. . . .

⅓ cup red wine vinegar
1 teaspoon chopped fresh ginger
1 teaspoon chopped garlic
Salt and pepper
1 cup olive oil
2 teaspoons black sesame seeds
   or toasted white sesame seeds

Makes 1½ cups

. . . .

· In a mixing bowl or blender, combine the vinegar, ginger, garlic, and salt and pepper to taste. Mix well and slowly add the olive oil and then the sesame seeds. If using a blender, add the olive oil in a drizzle with the blender on slow speed, but stir in the sesame seeds after transferring mixture to a jar or bowl. Refrigerate until ready to use.

*Here is an unusual way to use a
part of the papaya that is usually
discarded. Serve this with salad or
use as a marinade for chicken or
fish before grilling.*

PAPAYA SEED DRESSING

. . . .

Seeds from ½ medium papaya
¼ cup white wine vinegar
2 teaspoons sugar
Salt and pepper
2 teaspoons sour cream
1 cup vegetable oil

Makes 1½ cups

. . . .

· Wash the papaya seeds in a strainer until all are free of fruit pulp. Pat dry between 2 layers of paper towel.
· In a blender, place the vinegar, sugar, salt, and pepper. Blend until ingredients are dissolved. Add the sour cream and papaya seeds and mix. At a low speed, slowly incorporate the vegetable oil. Finish the dressing by seasoning with salt and pepper to taste. It will keep in the refrigerator for a few days.

This dressing is good on almost any salad.

ROASTED CASHEW DRESSING

· In a mixing bowl, combine the vinegar, ginger, and garlic and blend well. Stir in the honey, fish sauce, and soy sauce. Add the peanut oil, drop by drop, stirring constantly so the mixture emulsifies (like mayonnaise), followed by the sesame oil. Stir in the nuts and store in the refrigerator until ready to use.

. . . .

¼ cup balsamic vinegar

1 teaspoon minced fresh ginger

1 teaspoon minced garlic

1 teaspoon honey

1 teaspoon fish sauce

1 teaspoon light soy sauce

⅔ cup peanut oil

1 tablespoon roasted sesame oil

¼ cup chopped roasted cashews

Makes about 1 cup

. . . .

Scallop and Tobiko Ravioli
with Lime-Ginger Sauce

Serve this sauce with the Scallop and Tobiko Ravioli (page 25) or with any grilled or steamed fish.

· In a saucepan, combine the wine and ginger, bring to a boil, reduce the heat, and cook until reduced by one third.

· Add the cream and reduce by one third again.

· Over low heat, add the butter slowly, stirring constantly and adding a new piece as each piece is incorporated. Be careful not to let the sauce boil, as it will separate. Add the lime juice, and season with salt and pepper. The sauce can be prepared 1 hour in advance and kept in a simmering water bath or in a thermos.

$\mathcal{L}$IME-GINGER SAUCE

. . . .

¾ cup dry white wine

2 ½ teaspoons minced
   fresh ginger

½ cup heavy cream

1 cup (2 sticks) cold unsalted
   butter, cut in small pieces

Juice of 1 lime

Salt and pepper

Makes about 2 cups

. . . .

Serve this flavorful relish with Grilled Cured Nairagi with Sesame Tahini (page 35).

RILLED PINEAPPLE–FRESH CORIANDER RELISH

. . . .

4 1½-inch slices fresh pineapple
    with peel
½ cup chopped fresh coriander
1 garlic clove, minced
2 teaspoons minced fresh ginger
1 teaspoon rice vinegar
1 teaspoon fish sauce

Makes 1¼ cups

. . . .

· Grill or roast the pineapple slices and let cool. Remove peel and cut flesh into small cubes. Place in a mixing bowl with the coriander, garlic, ginger, vinegar, and fish sauce. Mix well and chill in the refrigerator until ready to serve.

Serve this tangy, lowfat dip with Deep-Fried Smoked Chicken Lumpia (page 53).

CURRIED LIME DIP

. . . .

3 teaspoons yellow curry powder
Juice of 1½ limes
Dash of cayenne pepper
½ teaspoon ground ginger
1 cup plain yogurt
Salt and pepper

Makes 1¼ cups

. . . .

· In a bowl, combine the curry powder, lime juice, cayenne pepper, and ginger. Mix well. Incorporate yogurt slowly into mixture. Season with salt and pepper to taste. Let sit for 1 hour before serving, to allow the flavor to develop.

Sauces and Relishes

· In a blender, combine the egg yolk with the garlic, chili paste, vinegar, and salt. Mix well. With the blender on slow speed, add the lemon juice and peanut oil until the dressing is blended. Refrigerate until ready to use.

This dressing is good on any salad. Try adding a little Parmesan cheese and serving on a Caesar Salad.

THAI DRESSING

. . . .

1 egg yolk
1 teaspoon chopped garlic
1 teaspoon red chili paste
¼ cup white wine vinegar
Salt
Juice of 1 lemon
⅔ cup peanut oil

Makes 1 cup

. . . .

Serve this Peanut Dip with
Vietnamese Spring Rolls
(page 56).

PEANUT DIP

. . . .

1 cup coconut milk

1 teaspoon fish sauce

⅔ teaspoon finely chopped garlic

1⅓ cups smooth-style peanut
    butter

2 teaspoons red curry paste
    (page 216)

Makes approximately 2 cups

. . . .

· In a large mixing bowl, combine the coconut milk, fish sauce, garlic, peanut butter, and curry paste until blended smoothly. Transfer to an airtight jar and store in the refrigerator until ready to use.

Steamed Vietnamese Spring

Rolls with Peanut Dip

This chutney is a modification of the classical Indian-style Tomato Chutney. I really like yellow and purple mustard seeds when they are sautéed—they bring an earthy flavor to the food and remind me of popcorn when they burst open. It is wonderful with Tempura-Style Soft Shell Crabs (page 85).

ᴛOMATO-GINGER-CORIANDER CHUTNEY

. . . .

2 tablespoons vegetable oil

3 tablespoons yellow
   mustard seeds

3 tablespoons purple
   mustard seeds

2 teaspoons chopped fresh ginger

1 minced garlic clove

½ cup chopped Maui onions

1 teaspoon cumin seeds

1½ teaspoons fennel seeds

2 cups diced, seeded tomato

¼ cup chopped fresh coriander

1 tablespoon red wine vinegar

Juice of 1 lemon

Makes about 1 cup

. . . .

·In a nonreactive saucepan over medium heat, sauté the mustard seeds in the oil for about half a minute. Add the ginger and garlic and sauté for about 15 seconds. Add the onion, cumin, fennel, and cook for about 3 minutes. Add the tomato and mix throughly. Cook over low heat for about 15 minutes, stirring often. Add the coriander, vinegar, and lemon juice and remove from heat. This chutney can be stored in the refrigerator for several days or may be served warm.

You can serve this chutney warm or chilled. It is an excellent accompaniment to lamb, pork, and shellfish. I also like to serve it with kamanu (rainbow runner) or kajiki (Pacific blue marlin).

MANGO-COCONUT CHUTNEY

· Soak the raisins in the rum for at least 1 hour. In the meantime, peel and chop the mangos, then season them with salt and pepper, and set aside.

· In a medium, nonreactive saucepan over medium heat, melt the butter and sauté the mango and garlic. Add the brown sugar, the malt vinegar, and the kumquat zest. Cook, covered, for about 5 minutes over low heat.

· Add the allspice, cumin, and ginger and cook for another 20 minutes. Add the raisins, coconut, and rum, and cook to thicken for another 5 minutes.

· Transfer to pint jars and seal. Allow to cool before refrigerating. The chutney will keep in the refrigerator for weeks.

. . . .

¾ cup golden raisins

¾ cup light rum

6 large ripe mangos

Salt and pepper

2 teaspoons unsalted butter

1½ teaspoons chopped garlic

3 cups light brown sugar

3 cups malt vinegar

¼ cup kumquat zest

1 teaspoon ground allspice

1 teaspoon ground cumin

½ cup chopped fresh ginger

1½ cups chopped coconut

Makes 2 pints

. . . .

Serve this refreshing salsa with
Peppered Ono Salad (page 38).

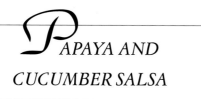APAYA AND CUCUMBER SALSA

. . . .

1 cup diced papaya, not too ripe
1 cup diced cucumber
2 teaspoons minced garlic
2 teaspoons minced fresh ginger
8 shredded mint leaves
4 teaspoons chopped fresh
   coriander
Juice of 2 lemons
½ fresh red chili pepper, minced
½ medium Maui onion, minced

Makes about 2½ cups

. . . .

· In a mixing bowl, combine the diced papaya and cucumber. Add the garlic and ginger and mix well. Add the remaining ingredients, folding them in gently.

The poha is a yellow-green berry about the size of a cherry, enclosed in a papery husk. It is also known as a cape gooseberry, husk tomato, and ground cherry. The poha is waxy on the outside but juicy inside, with many tiny seeds. Serve these preserves with Banana Buttermilk Pancakes (page 194), macadamia waffles, or just on warm toast.

OHA PRESERVES

. . . .

6 cups poha berries, husked
1 cup water
5 cups sugar
Juice of 3 lemons
1 tablespoon minced fresh ginger

Makes 2¹/₂ cups

. . . .

· In a saucepan, combine the poha berries and water and slowly bring to a boil. Reduce the heat and simmer for about 20 minutes, stirring frequently, until there is just enough liquid to prevent the fruit from scorching. Remove from the heat and refrigerate overnight.

· Return the fruit to the stove and add the sugar, lemon juice, and ginger. Cook gently for another 30 minutes, until the fruit is soft. Cool, place in hot sterilized jars, cover, and refrigerate. The preserves will keep for months in the refrigerator.

Serve this sauce with Steamed New Zealand Green Mussels (page 34).

RED CURRY–COCONUT SAUCE

½ cup dry white wine
1 teaspoon chopped fresh ginger
2 teaspoons chopped garlic
½ cup clam juice
2 cups coconut milk
2 tablespoons red curry paste
  (page 216)
Juice of 1 lime
¼ cup julienned basil leaves
Salt

Makes 2 cups

· In a nonreactive saucepan, combine the wine, ginger, and garlic, and bring to a boil.
· Add the clam juice and coconut milk, and return the mixture to a boil, stirring in the curry paste. Cook gently until well dissolved, about 10 minutes. Add the lemon juice, basil, and salt to taste. Refrigerate until ready to use.

Steamed New Zealand

Green Mussels with

Red Curry—Coconut Sauce

*This spicy sauce is my personal
favorite. It can be served with all
types of fish and shellfish.*

ED CURRY–
COCONUT-BASIL SAUCE

. . . .

½ cup dry white wine
⅓ cup fish stock or clam juice
⅔ cup coconut milk
1 stalk lemongrass, thinly sliced
1 teaspoon sliced kaffir lime leaf
2 tablespoons cornstarch mixed
    with ⅓ cup cold water
Juice of 2 limes
2 teaspoons red curry paste
    (page 216)
6 basil leaves, sliced

Makes 2 cups

. . . .

· Place the wine in a large nonreactive saucepan and reduce by two thirds over medium heat. Add the stock or clam juice, bring the mixture to a boil, and add the coconut milk. Return the liquid to a boil and add the lemongrass and lime leaf. Simmer for 15 minutes.
· Add the cornstarch mixture and simmer for another 5 minutes, until the sauce is thick enough to coat the back of a spoon. Add the lime juice, curry paste, and basil leaves. (You can add more curry paste if you like it hot—or a little less if you like things a bit milder, though the paste helps bring out the other flavors.)

*Japan meets France in this
unusual sauce. Serve it with
Crisp Shiitake Polenta (page 46).*

ASABE-SOY
BEURRE BLANC

. . . .

1 cup dry white wine
½ cup heavy cream
1 cup (2 sticks) unsalted butter,
    chilled and cut into pieces
½ teaspoon prepared wasabe
    (Japanese horseradish)
2 teaspoons dark soy sauce

Makes 1¼ cups

. . . .

· In a saucepan over medium heat, reduce the wine by two thirds. Add the cream and reduce by two thirds. While stirring constantly with a whisk, incorporate the butter, a few pieces at a time, without letting the sauce boil, until all the butter is incorporated. Add the wasabe and soy sauce.

· In a mixing bowl, combine the avocado, chili pepper, coriander, tomatoes, sesame seeds, garlic, onion, and pepper. Mix gently until all the ingredients are combined.

· Season to taste with the salt and add the sesame oil, mixing gently. Refrigerate until ready to serve.

Serve with Barbecued Yellowfin Tuna (page 113).

AVOCADO RELISH

. . . .

1 small ripe, firm avocado, peeled
   and cut into small cubes

1 teaspoon minced fresh
   chili pepper

¼ cup chopped fresh coriander

2 ripe medium tomatoes, peeled,
   seeded, and diced

3 teaspoons toasted white
   sesame seeds

1 teaspoon minced garlic

1 small sweet onion, diced

¼ red bell pepper, diced

Salt

1 teaspoon roasted sesame oil

Makes 1¾ cups

. . . .

Steamed Pork and Shrimp
Suimai with Teriyaki Dip

This tangy sauce will keep in the refrigerator for months. It is especially good with Steamed Pork and Shrimp Suimai (page 57).

TERIYAKI DIP

· In a small bowl, combine the soy sauce, sugar, garlic, ginger, miso, sake, and sesame seeds. Set aside until ready to use.

. . . .

1 cup soy sauce

⅓ cup sugar

1 garlic clove, crushed

2 teaspoons freshly grated ginger

½ teaspoon miso

⅓ cup sake

1 teaspoon toasted white sesame seeds

Makes 1½ cups

. . . .

Crab shells contain a lot of flavor,
so use them to make this tasty
sauce. It is great with Samoan
Crab Meat Ravioli (page 81).

CRAB-LEMONGRASS SAUCE

. . . .

5 ounces crab shells and legs
2 tablespoons olive oil
1 medium carrot
1 medium red onion
3 button mushrooms
1 teaspoon paprika
6 garlic cloves
4 stalks fresh lemongrass, diced
1 cup dry white wine
1½ cups fish stock or clam juice
2 teaspoons tomato paste
2 teaspoons fish sauce
Pinch of cayenne pepper
4 tablespoons (½ stick)
   unsalted butter
Freshly ground black pepper

Makes 1¼ cups

. . . .

· Cut the crab shells and legs into pieces. In a saucepan, heat the olive oil over medium heat and sauté the shells and legs for about 2 minutes over high heat, until they are lightly brown. Add the carrot, onion, mushrooms, paprika, garlic, and lemongrass. Cook for 2 minutes, then add the wine, stir, and reduce liquid by two thirds.

· Add the fish stock, reduce cooking liquid for 5 minutes, and add the tomato paste, fish sauce, and cayenne. Reduce for 5 minutes more, then strain the mixture and return it to the pan. Bring sauce back to a boil and add the butter and pepper to taste. Keep warm.

Ama ebi, or sweet shrimp, are
easy to recognize by their long
antennae and deep reddish color.
If not available, use blue crab
or shrimp shells. Serve this sauce
with Seared Ulua with Mushroom Cannelloni (page 92).

$\mathcal{S}$WEET AMA EBI SAUCE

· Heat the oil in a saucepan over medium heat. Add the shrimp shells and sauté for 2 minutes, or until the shells turn golden. Add the onion, carrot, garlic, and tomato paste and sauté for 2 minutes more.

· Deglaze with the wine, and reduce for 1 minute at a simmer. Add the fish stock, cayenne, paprika, ginger, and thyme. Bring to a boil and simmer for about 20 minutes.

· Pass through a strainer, return to a boil, and simmer for another 5 minutes. Remove any oil from the surface with a ladle. Keep in a warm place until ready to serve.

. . . .

¼ cup olive oil

3 cups shells of ama ebi or shrimp

1 medium onion, chopped

1 medium carrot, chopped

2 teaspoons minced garlic

2 tablespoons tomato paste

½ cup dry white wine

4 cups fish stock or clam juice

Pinch of cayenne pepper

1 teaspoon paprika

2 teaspoons minced fresh ginger

2 sprigs fresh thyme

Makes 2 cups

. . . .

Wonton Chips and Charred

Scallops with Hawaiian Pesto

Ginger, scallions, and fresh coriander give this pesto a distinctly Hawaiian taste. Serve it with Wonton Chips and Charred Scallops (page 48).

$\mathcal{H}$AWAIIAN PESTO

· In a small bowl combine the ginger, scallions, coriander, and garlic. In a saucepan, heat the peanut and sesame oils until they are hot; pour the oils over the ginger mixture. Add the salt and pepper, lemon juice, and Parmesan cheese and mix well. Refrigerate until ready to use.

. . . .

½ cup chopped fresh ginger
½ cup chopped scallions
½ cup chopped fresh coriander
1 teaspoon chopped garlic
½ cup peanut oil
2 teaspoons sesame oil
Salt and freshly ground
   white pepper
Juice of 1 lemon
2 teaspoons grated
   Parmesan cheese

Makes 1½ cups

. . . .

Serve this sauce with grilled shell-fish or seared or blackened fish.

 NNATTO-GINGER SAUCE

. . . .

2 cups dry white wine

1 tablespoon chopped fresh ginger

1 cup heavy cream

1 cup (2 sticks) unsalted butter

3 teaspoons annatto powder

Makes 1 cup

. . . .

· Place the wine in a nonreactive saucepan over medium heat and add the ginger. Cook until the wine is reduced by two thirds. Add the cream and reduce again by two thirds. Slowly whisk in the butter until completely incorporated. Stir in the annatto powder and blend for 20 seconds in a blender. Store in a thermos until ready to use.

This pesto's strong flavor and chunky consistency make it a little different from other pestos. Use as a dip or as a condiment for raw fish like ahi.

 INGER-SCALLION PESTO

. . . .

1 teaspoon chopped garlic

½ cup chopped fresh ginger

½ cup chopped scallions

¼ cup chopped salted
   macadamia nuts

White pepper

½ cup olive oil

Makes 1 ¼ cups

. . . .

· In a mixing bowl, combine the garlic, ginger, scallions, macadamia nuts, and pepper to taste. Slowly incorporate the olive oil and continue whisking until the mixture forms a paste.

· Transfer to a container and store, covered, in the refrigerator until ready to use.

*This is a great salad dressing,
but you can also serve it with
fish or lamb chops or use it as
a marinade for chicken.*

CHILLED GINGER DRESSING

. . . .

1/2 cup minced fresh ginger
1/4 cup chopped scallions
1/4 cup minced fresh shallots
1/4 cup minced fresh coriander
1/4 cup peanut oil
1/4 cup olive oil
I teaspoon roasted sesame oil
Pinch of salt

Makes 1 1/2 cups

. . . .

· In a mixing bowl, combine the ginger, scallions, shallots,
and coriander.

· In a saucepan, heat the peanut, olive, and sesame oils and the
salt until hot. Remove from the heat and combine with the
ginger mixture. Stir well and refrigerate until ready to use.

*Serve this classic sauce with
Sizzling Ginger Mahi-Mahi
(page 102).*

SHABU DIPPING SAUCE

. . . .

1/4 cup fish stock
I teaspoon fish sauce
5 tablespoons light soy sauce
I tablespoon mirin (sweet
    rice wine)
I teaspoon rice vinegar
Toasted white sesame seeds or
    minced fresh garlic (optional)

Makes approximately 1/2 cup

. . . .

· Combine the fish stock, fish sauce, soy sauce, mirin, vinegar,
and sesame seeds or garlic (if desired) and mix well.

Serve this relish with Wok-Seared
Fish and Shrimp Cakes (page 78).

OGO-TOMATO RELISH

. . . .

2 medium tomatoes, peeled,
   seeded, and diced
1 cup ogo (fresh seaweed)
1 small onion, finely diced
2 teaspoons black sesame seeds
Juice of 1 lime
Pinch of salt
4 snow peas, sliced
2 teaspoons red wine vinegar
6 teaspoons olive oil

Makes 2 1/2 cups

. . . .

· In a medium mixing bowl combine the tomatoes, ogo, onion, sesame seeds, lime juice, salt, snow peas, vinegar, and olive oil and mix well. Refrigerate until ready to serve.

Serve this tangy vinaigrette with
Seared Opah with Vegetable
Relish (page 112).

ANNATTO VINAIGRETTE

. . . .

3 tablespoons red wine vinegar
Salt and pepper
3 teaspoons ground annatto
2 teaspoons minced ginger
1 teaspoon minced garlic
Juice of 1 lime
1/2 cup vegetable oil

Makes 1 cup

. . . .

· In a blender at medium speed, combine the vinegar, salt and pepper, and annatto. Blend for about 10 seconds, then add the ginger, garlic, and lime juice. Slowly add the oil in a thin stream. Reserve until ready to use.

Select the freshest corn and the sweetest onions possible to make this zesty relish.

GRILLED CORN AND MAUI ONION RELISH

· Prepare the grill.

· Cut the onion in ¼-inch-thick slices and brush with vegetable oil. Grill for about 2 minutes on each side and set aside. Chop when cool.

· At the same time place the corn, in their husks, on the grill. Grill for about 20 minutes, turning them every 3 minutes. Remove from the grill and let cool for 10 minutes. The husks can then be removed and discarded.

· Cut the corn kernels from the cobs. In a mixing bowl, combine the corn, onion, coriander, chili pepper, bell pepper, sage, and chili powder. Mix in the vinegar, remaining vegetable oil, and lemon juice, and let sit until ready to use. This relish should be served at room temperature.

. . . .

1 medium Maui onion

¼ cup vegetable oil

2 ears of corn, in husks with
    silks removed

¼ cup fresh coriander, chopped

1 small red chili pepper, chopped

½ medium red bell pepper, diced

4 sage leaves, chopped

¼ teaspoon chili powder

2 tablespoons red wine vinegar

2 tablespoons lemon juice

Makes 2½ cups

. . . .

This dressing combines the flavors of tart apples, ginger, and lime juice. When selecting ginger, press it with your thumb to make sure it's not dry. It should be soft and juicy.

GREEN APPLE DRESSING

. . . .

1 green apple, cored and chopped
Juice of 2 limes
½ cup white wine vinegar
3 teaspoons ginger juice
　　(see Note)
1 teaspoon dark soy sauce
Salt and freshly ground
　　white pepper
1⅓ cups vegetable oil

Makes 2⅓ cups

. . . .

· Place the apple and lime juice in a blender and puree. Add the vinegar, ginger juice, and soy sauce, and mix well. Add the salt and pepper. Slowly incorporate the oil, blending a little at a time until well combined.

· Note: Ginger juice can be extracted from fresh ginger in a juice extractor (1 cup chopped ginger will yield ¼ cup juice). If you don't have one, you can also use a garlic press. Ginger juice is a flavorful addition to cookie doughs and stir-fried dishes.

Serve this sweet, highly flavored syrup with pancakes or waffles. My little girl, Leilani, loves ice cream with fresh fruit and this syrup.

GUAVA SYRUP

· In a heavy saucepan, combine the guava juice, water, and sugar. Slowly bring the mixture to a boil, then reduce the heat slightly and cook, stirring occasionally, until a syrup forms, about 20 to 30 minutes. Cool and place in hot sterilized jars. This syrup will keep for a couple of weeks in the refrigerator.

1 cup guava juice

1 cup water

1 cup sugar

Makes about 2 cups

7

Breads and Sweets

This is one of my daughter's favorites. The pancakes never last very long on her plate, and I don't really mind cleaning the syrup off her clothes. • This recipe can also be made with other tropical fruits like papaya or pineapple. Serve with Guava Syrup (page 191), pineapple sauce, or strawberry sauce.

*B*ANANA
BUTTERMILK PANCAKES

. . . .

1⅔ cups all-purpose flour

3 teaspoons baking powder

Pinch of salt

2 cups buttermilk

4 eggs, separated

½ teaspoon cream of tartar

¼ cup (½ stick) unsalted butter, melted

1 cup sliced banana or other fruit

Serves 4

. . . .

· Preheat a griddle or nonstick frying pan.

· In a mixing bowl, briefly combine the flour, baking powder, and salt. In another bowl, combine the buttermilk and egg yolks. Whip the egg whites in a mixer until foamy. Add the cream of tartar and whip until soft peaks begin to form.

· Combine the flour and yolk mixtures and stir in the melted butter. The batter should now be a little lumpy. Fold in the egg whites with a spatula.

· Brush the griddle or skillet with butter and add some batter. Add about 6 banana slices per pancake and cook 1 minute on each side.

- Preheat the oven to 450°F.
- In a mixer bowl, combine the flour, sugar, baking soda, salt, poppy seeds, and sesame seeds. Mix at low speed with the bread hook for about 2 minutes.
- Incorporate the butter and buttermilk. Keep the dough covered with a cloth.
- Take balls of dough about the size of oranges and roll into thin rectangular sheets. Line a baking sheet with wax paper and place the rectangular dough on top of it.
- Bake until dough turns light brown. Let cool on a rack. Lavosh will keep for 3 days if stored at room temperature in a plastic container.

Lavosh is an unleavened bread that originated in Armenia. Dusting the bowl with flour will facilitate the removal of the dough.

$\mathcal{L}$AVOSH

. . . .

3 cups bread flour

2 tablespoons sugar

½ teaspoon baking soda

¼ teaspoon salt

1 tablespoon poppy seeds

1 tablespoon white sesame seeds

½ cup (1 stick) unsalted
butter, softened

1 cup buttermilk

Serves 4–6

. . . .

Imagine yourself on a Hawaiian Island, looking at the sunset, drinking a cup of kona coffee, and eating a slice of White Chocolate–Guava Cake with the sound of steel guitars in the background. It's paradise!

White Chocolate– Guava Cake with Roasted Banana Cream Sauce

. . . .

- *Custard*

  3 egg yolks

  1/3 cup heavy cream

  1/3 cup milk

  1/3 cup sugar

  1/2 vanilla bean, split

  5 ounces grated white chocolate

. . . .

- *Cake Batter*

  3/4 cup unsalted butter,
     at room temperature

  1 cup sugar

  2 eggs, at room temperature

  1 cup flour, sifted

  1 teaspoon baking powder

  1/2 teaspoon salt

  1/3 cup milk

  1/3 cup pureed ripe guava

. . . .

- *Roasted Banana Cream Sauce*

  2 medium ripe bananas

  2 tablespoons sugar

  2 tablespoons dark rum,
     preferably Hana Bay

  1 teaspoon vanilla extract

  2/3 cup heavy cream

  Roasted banana slices, for garnish
  White chocolate curls, for garnish

Serves 8

. . . .

- In top of double boiler combine egg yolks, cream, milk, sugar, and vanilla bean. Cook over gently simmering water until custard is thick enough to coat the back of a wooden spoon. Remove from heat and discard vanilla bean. Stir in white chocolate. Let cool completely.
- Preheat the oven to 325°F. Grease and flour the bottom of a 9×2-inch round cake pan. Set aside.
- In a large bowl with electric mixer, beat butter and sugar until light and fluffy. Beat in eggs, one at a time, and continue beating for 5 minutes. On lowest speed, beat in the cooled custard. Combine flour, baking powder, and salt.
- In measuring cup, combine milk and guava puree. On lowest speed, add flour mixture and milk mixture alternately, beginning and ending with the dry ingredients and beating just until combined. Pour into prepared pan. Bake 1 hour and 15 minutes, until the cake is deep golden brown and a wooden toothpick inserted into the center of the cake comes out clean. Let cool 10 minutes. Invert the cake onto a wire rack, then invert again so that the cake cools right side up. Let cool completely. Serve garnished with Roasted Banana Cream Sauce, roasted banana slices, and white chocolate curls.

- *Roasted Banana Cream Sauce*
- Preheat the oven to 350°F.
- Place 2 unpeeled bananas on the middle rack of your oven and bake for 15 minutes, or until soft. Let cool to lukewarm. Peel the roasted bananas and place their flesh in a blender. Add the sugar, rum, and vanilla and blend briefly. Add the heavy cream and blend again. The mixture should have the consistency of a puree. Store in the refrigerator until ready to serve.

This classic sponge cake becomes an elegant dessert with the tropical flavors of coconut and guava.

. . . .

- *C a k e*

  1 ¼ cups sifted cake flour

  ½ cup sugar

  Pinch of salt

  1 tablespoon baking powder

  3 tablespoons vegetable oil

  3 eggs

  4 tablespoons water

  4 egg whites

  Pinch of cream of tartar

. . . .

*C*OCONUT CAKE WITH GUAVA PASTRY CREAM

. . . .

- *G u a v a   P a s t r y   C r e a m*

  1 ¼ cups milk

  ½ cup guava juice

  6 egg yolks

  ⅓ cup sugar

  ⅓ cup all-purpose flour

  ½ cup whipped cream

. . . .

- *G a r n i s h*

  ½ cup whipped cream

  ½ cup Guava Syrup (page 191) or guava juice

  1 ½ cups toasted coconut flakes

  Serves 8

. . . .

· Preheat the oven to 350°F.

· In a mixing bowl, sift together the cake flour, ⅓ cup sugar, salt, and baking powder. In another mixing bowl, combine the oil, eggs, and water. Combine the contents of both bowls until the batter is smooth.

· With an electric mixer, whip the egg whites and cream of tartar, gradually adding the remaining sugar until the mixture forms a stiff meringue. Fold in the coconut flakes. Fold the batter into the meringue mixture.

· Pour the mixture into a 9-inch springform pan and bake for 25 to 30 minutes, or until a knife inserted into the center comes out clean. Remove from the pan and let cool on a rack.

· Bring the milk and guava juice to a boil in a saucepan. In a mixing bowl, combine the eggs with the sugar. Slowly add the flour and mix thoroughly to avoid lumps. Add a third of the hot milk mixture to the egg-and-sugar mixture and whisk well. Pour this mixture into the remaining milk and guava juice and cook over medium heat, stirring constantly with a wooden spoon until it thickens and is completely cooked, taking care that it doesn't scorch or curdle.

· Remove from heat and transfer to a mixing bowl. Put plastic wrap directly on top of the pastry cream to prevent a skin from forming. Let cool completely. Just before you assemble the cake, combine the pastry cream with ½ cup of whipped cream. Store in the refrigerator until ready to use.

· When the cake has completely cooled, cut it into 3 equal layers. Place the bottom layer on a flat plate and brush with guava syrup. Spread a third of the pastry cream mixture over it and sprinkle with coconut flakes. Repeat until all layers are filled.

· Frost the outside of the cake with the whipped cream, and sprinkle with coconut flakes.

- Preheat the oven to 350°F. Grease a 9×13-inch cake pan.
- Pour the lime and lemon juice over the banana slices. Add the lemon zest and macerate the bananas for about 15 minutes.
- In a saucepan, melt the butter with the brown sugar. Spoon the bananas evenly over the bottom of the cake pan and pour the butter and brown sugar mixture carefully over them.
- Cream the butter and sugar for the cake. Add the eggs. In a separate bowl, sift together the flour, baking powder, and salt. Add dry ingredients to sugar mixture, alternating with the milk as you incorporate them into the mixture. Pour batter over the bananas in the cake pan and bake for 45 minutes. When the cake is done, run a knife around the edges to loosen it and invert the pan over your serving dish. Serve it warm or at room temperature.

There are many varieties of bananas available in Hawaii. One of the most common is the Bluefields, a smooth yellow banana with creamy white flesh and a mild flavor. We also have Brazilian bananas, called apple bananas in Hawaii. They are about the size of a finger, with firm flesh and a tart taste. There are also bananas that must be cooked to be eaten. Populu are short and thick, with a light-pink-colored flesh that turns light yellow when cooked. Maiamaoli are also pink, but larger. They are excellent broiled or baked.

BANANA
UPSIDE-DOWN CAKE

- *Topping*
  Juice of 1 lime
  Juice of 1 lemon
  2 cups sliced ripe banana
  1 teaspoon minced lemon zest
  1 tablespoon unsalted butter
  ½ cup light brown sugar
- *Cake*
  ¼ cup (½ stick) unsalted butter
  ⅔ cup superfine sugar
  2 eggs, beaten
  1½ cups all-purpose flour
  1½ teaspoons baking powder
  Pinch of salt
  ½ cup milk

  Serves 8–12

This is a refreshing dessert. Be
sure to use ripe pineapples. In
Hawaii, we can get miniature
pineapples, which are about four
inches high and make a pleasing
presentation. If they are unavailable, fill a shallow bowl or cup
with diced pineapple, and cover
with the custard.

PINEAPPLE-GINGER CREME BRULEE

. . . .

10 egg yolks

1 cup + 3 tablespoons
granulated sugar

4 cups heavy cream

1 teaspoon vanilla extract

2 teaspoons ground ginger

8 fresh pineapples

Serves 8

. . . .

· Mix the egg yolks and 3 tablespoons of sugar in the top of a double boiler. Set it over simmering water and beat the mixture vigorously and continuously until it forms a ribbon. The egg yolks must be cooked thoroughly, but should never get hot enough to scramble. (You should always be able to put your finger into the mixture without burning yourself.)

· Scald the cream and add the vanilla and ginger. Fold slowly into the egg mixture and cook over simmering water for 30 to 40 minutes, stirring every so often.

· In the meantime, cut the tops off the pineapples and care- fully remove the fruit, discarding the core and cutting the flesh into small cubes. Put the fruit back into the shells and cover with the custard all the way to the top. Refrigerate for 2 to 3 hours until set and well chilled.

· When ready to serve, sprinkle the custard with the remain- ing cup of sugar and caramelize with a gas torch or in a broiler. The caramel will harden when it cools.

*Mango Bread is good for break-
fast, school lunches, snacks, or
as a dessert with ice cream.*

$\mathcal{M}$ANGO BREAD

. . . .

2 cups all-purpose flour

2 teaspoons baking soda

1 teaspoon ground cinnamon

¹/₂ teaspoon salt

1¹/₂ cups sugar

4 eggs

¹/₄ cup chopped macadamia nuts

¹/₄ cup walnuts, broken in pieces

³/₄ cup vegetable oil

2 cups ripe mango, cut in
   small cubes

Makes 1 9×5-inch loaf

. . . .

· Preheat the oven to 350°F. Grease a 9×5-inch loaf pan.
· In a mixing bowl, combine flour, baking soda, cinnamon, and salt. Form a well in the center of the mixture and add sugar, eggs, macadamia nuts, walnuts, and oil. Add mango and slowly incorporate into the flour mixture.
· Pour ingredients into a loaf pan and bake for 45 minutes, or until a knife inserted into the center comes out clean.

- Preheat oven to 325°F.
- Beat the egg yolks in the top of a double-boiler over hot water until very thick. Gradually beat in ½ cup superfine sugar. Stir in the passion fruit juice and mint leaves and keep cooking until the mixture coats the back of a spoon. Strain and allow to cool.
- With a mixer, blend the egg whites with the salt until soft peaks form. Gradually add the rest of the sugar and whip until stiff. Fold a third of the egg white mixture into the yolks. Mix thoroughly, then add the rest of the whites by folding in gently. Pour the mixture into the pie shell and bake for 15 minutes. Cool before serving.

- *Sugar Tart Pastry*
  - Combine the flour, salt, and sugar in a mixing bowl. Cut the butter into small pieces and add to the mixture, working it by hand until well blended.
  - Add the water little by little, working the dough by hand for 1 minute until it holds together well. It should not be wet or sticky. Place in a plastic bag and refrigerate for about 1 hour.
  - Preheat the oven to 375°F.
  - On a lightly floured table roll the dough to about a ⅛-inch thickness. Place in a pie mold, pinching it along the sides of the mold. Cover the pastry with aluminum foil and weigh it down with beans or pastry weights so that it will not bubble.
  - Bake for about 20 minutes or until the middle of the pastry shell is slightly golden.

Lilikoi *is the Hawaiian word for passion fruit. It is native to Brazil but commonly grown in Hawaii, where both a purple and a yellow variety are available. The fruit can be found frozen in Asian groceries.*

*L*ILIKOI MINT CHIFFON PIE

. . . .

5 eggs, separated
¾ cup superfine sugar
⅔ cup passion fruit (lilikoi) juice
6 mint leaves, sliced
Pinch of salt
1 9-inch pie shell made from
   Sugar Tart Pastry

Serves 6–8

. . . .

- *Sugar Tart Pastry*
  2½ cups all-purpose flour
  1 pinch salt
  ½ cup sugar
  1 cup (2 sticks) unsalted butter
  ¼ cup ice water

  *Makes 1 9- to 11-inch pie
  or tart shell*

. . . .

This rustic tart has roots in France, but I couldn't resist giving it a Hawaiian twist.

. . . .

- *Tart*

   1½ cups (3 sticks) unsalted butter
   ½ vanilla bean
   1 cup sugar
   12 medium pears
   Juice of 2 lemons
   1 9-inch tart shell made with
      Sugar Tart Pastry (page 203)

. . . .

OLD-FASHIONED PEAR TART WITH VANILLA– MACADAMIA NUT ICE CREAM

. . . .

- *Ice Cream*

   1½ cups milk
   3 cups heavy cream
   2 tablespoons macadamia
      nut liqueur
   8 egg yolks
   ½ cup sugar
   ⅔ cup roasted macadamia nuts

   Serves 6–8

. . . .

· Preheat the oven to 350°F.

· Melt the butter over medium heat in an 11-inch cast-iron skillet. Scrape the inside of the vanilla bean and add to the butter. Then add the sugar and whisk until ingredients are well blended.

· Peel the pears, slice them in half, and remove their cores. Place them in a mixing bowl with the lemon juice to prevent them from turning brown.

· Place the pears core side up in concentric circles in the skillet, going around the outside of the skillet first. It is important that the pears fit snugly in the skillet. Plug up any holes with pear slices if necessary.

· Cook the pears over medium heat. They will lose some of their liquid and become soft; continue cooking until the liquid comes to a boil, then reduce to a simmer and cook until the liquid turns the color of caramel. Remove pan from heat and let the pears cool completely.

· Lightly dust a table with flour and roll the dough to about a ⅛-inch thickness. Cover the pears with the dough and bake for about 20 minutes or until dough is completely cooked. Remove from the oven and let cool.

· Place a large plate over the skillet and flip it upside down. The tart can be served warm or at room temperature.

- *Ice Cream*

· In a saucepan, scald the milk, cream, and liqueur. Remove from heat and put aside until ready to use.

· In a mixing bowl, combine the egg yolks and sugar. Whisk for about 3 minutes until the mixture lightens and forms ribbons. Then add a third of the milk mixture and whisk well. Return the contents of the bowl to the saucepan and whisk all the ingredients together. Cook over low heat for about 2 minutes or until the mixture coats the back of a wooden spoon.

· Strain the mixture through a fine strainer into a bowl set in a larger bowl of ice. When completely cool, transfer the contents to an ice cream maker and follow manufacturer's instructions. When the ice cream hardens, add the roasted macadamia nuts and serve.

*These chewy cookies are great to
serve with sorbet or ice cream, or
simply to eat at the beach.*

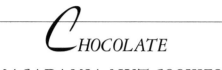

CHOCOLATE
MACADAMIA NUT COOKIES

. . . .

3 cups confectioners' sugar
7 teaspoons cocoa
2 teaspoons all-purpose flour
3 egg whites
8 ounces unsalted macadamia nuts

Makes 2 dozen

. . . .

· Preheat the oven to 350°F. Line 2 baking sheets with parchment paper.
· In a mixing bowl, combine the confectioners' sugar, cocoa, and flour. Add the egg whites and, with an electric beater, beat at medium speed for 2 minutes. Lower the speed and mix in the macadamia nuts.
· Drop batter by teaspoonfuls onto the parchment paper and bake for about 12 minutes, or until cookies are golden brown. Let the cookies cool on the parchment paper before removing.

*A local favorite, this sweet dump-
ling is full of flavors redolent of
the Philippines. Served on a stick,
it is great for the beach.*

PINEAPPLE COCONUT
CASCARON

. . . .

Oil, for frying
1½ cups mochiko (sweet
   rice) flour
2 cups water
½ cup milk
⅓ cup light brown sugar
3 cups grated coconut
1 cup cubed fresh pineapple
Granulated sugar or honey

Makes about 6 dozen

. . . .

· In a deep-fat fryer, heat the oil to 325° to 350°F.
· In a mixing bowl, combine the flour, water, milk, brown sugar, coconut, and pineapple and blend well.
· With a soup spoon, carefully drop spoonfuls of batter in the hot oil. Fry the dumplings a few at a time, turning them often, until they are golden all over, about 2 minutes on each side. Remove and drain on paper towels.
· Roll the dumplings in sugar or brush with honey. Serve them hot or at room temperature.

This tart can be made in a large tart pan or in individual tart pans. Topped with a caramelized meringue, it looks like the sleeping giant of Wailua, a natural rock formation in the mountains.

SLEEPING GIANT LEMON TART

. . . .

4 small tartlet shells or 1 11-inch
    tart shell made with Sugar
    Tart Pastry (page 203)
1 ⅓ cups milk
4 egg yolks
½ cup lemon juice
2 teaspoons grated lemon rind
7 teaspoons sugar
5 egg whites

Makes 4 tartlets or 1 large tart

. . . .

· Preheat the oven to 375°F. Prebake the tartlet shells for 6 minutes. Let cool but leave oven on.

· In a medium mixing bowl, combine the milk, egg yolks, lemon juice, lemon rind, and 4 teaspoons of the sugar. Pour into the tartlet shells and bake for approximately 20 minutes, or until set. Let the tartlets cool completely.

· When ready to serve, preheat the broiler. Whip the egg whites in a mixer or with a hand beater until almost stiff. Add the remaining sugar and beat until stiff. Spread the meringue on the tartlets and place under the broiler for 10 to 15 seconds to caramelize the sugar and brown the meringue.

Here I've combined a classic French cookie with Asian flavors. You can use macadamia nuts instead of sesame seeds, but be sure to chop them well.

SESAME TUILES WITH LILIKOI SORBET

. . . .

5 tablespoons (⅔ stick) unsalted
  butter, softened
½ teaspoon white sesame seeds
½ teaspoon lime zest
¼ cup sugar
2 egg whites
½ cup all-purpose flour
6 scoops Lilikoi Sorbet (page 210)
3 cups cut up fresh fruit, such as
  pineapple, papaya, banana,
  guava, kiwi, raspberries, or
  strawberries

Serves 6

. . . .

· Preheat the oven to 425°F. Grease a baking sheet.
· In a mixing bowl, combine the butter, sesame seeds, and lime zest with a spatula. Add the sugar and egg whites and fold in the flour.
· Drop batter by tablespoonfuls on the baking sheet. Flatten the batter with the rounded side of a spoon to form 6 circles about 4 inches in diameter. Bake for about 4 minutes or until the batter turns golden.
· With a spatula remove the cookies from the baking sheet. While still warm, gently press each over the top of a glass to form a cup. Let the tuiles cool completely before filling them with sorbet and fresh fruit.

Serve this ambrosial sorbet with fresh fruit in Sesame Tuiles (page 208).

LILIKOI SORBET

. . . .

2 cups water

1 cup sugar

1 cup passion fruit (lilikoi) juice

Serves 4–6

. . . .

· Bring 1 cup of water and the sugar to a boil. Once a syrup forms, let it cool.

· Combine the fruit juice and remaining water with the syrup, mixing well. Add the mixture to the ice cream maker and process according to manufacturer's instructions. Store in the freezer until ready to serve.

Kauai has one of the largest guava farms in the United States, Guava Kai.

GUAVA SORBET

. . . .

1 cup sugar

1½ cups water

1 cup guava juice

Serves 4–6

. . . .

· In a nonreactive saucepan, combine the sugar with ¾ cup water and bring to a boil. Once a syrup has formed, let it cool.

· Mix the guava juice with the remaining water and add to the syrup. Pour the mixture into an ice cream maker and follow the manufacturer's instructions.

- Peel and cut all the fruits into 1-inch cubes and place in a large mixing bowl. In a separate bowl, mix the pineapple juice, honey, lemon juice, and mint. Refrigerate until you are ready to serve the dessert.
- In a medium saucepan, combine the coconut milk and water and place over medium heat. Add a tablespoon or two of water to the cornstarch, stir to make a paste, and add the mixture to the coconut milk, stirring constantly. Add the sugar and vanilla bean or extract to the mixture and continue to cook over medium heat until thickened. When the mixture coats the back of a spoon, reduce the heat to a simmer and continue to cook for another 20 minutes, stirring often to avoid any lumps or scorching.
- Pour the mixture into an 8-inch-square pan and chill until set, at least 4 hours.
- When ready to serve, cut the haupia into squares. Put each square on a plate, add a serving of tropical fruit salad, and pour the pineapple juice mixture on top.

Haupia is a coconut custard dessert traditionally served at luaus. To add a little color— and some great flavor—I serve it with a tropical fruit salad. I get clove honey from a local beekeeper. If you can't find it, use any good honey.

HAUPIA WITH TROPICAL FRUIT SALAD

. . . .

1 medium mango
½ medium papaya
2 kiwi fruit
½ cup pineapple juice
½ cup clove honey
Juice of 1 lemon
6 mint leaves, julienned
¾ cup coconut milk, canned or
    frozen if fresh is not available
¾ cup water
⅔ cup cornstarch
⅔ cup sugar
½ vanilla bean or 2 teaspoons
    vanilla extract

Serves 6–8

. . . .

Appendix

*A good, strong chicken stock can be
made in about 45 minutes,
and once you taste it you will
never want to use canned stock,
bouillon cubes, or powder again.
You can freeze the stock in small
containers and pull them out of
the freezer as you need them.*

CHICKEN STOCK

. . . .

2 quarts cold water
1 medium chicken, cleaned and
    cut up
2 medium carrots
2 celery stalks
2 medium onions
Bouquet garni with fresh thyme
    and bay leaf
½ cup shiitake mushroom stems
3 teaspoons Hawaiian or
    coarse salt

Makes 2 quarts

. . . .

· Put chicken in a large pot and cover with the cold water. Bring the water to a gentle boil. With a ladle, carefully remove all scum from the surface until the water is free of any residue.
· Add the carrots, celery, onions, bouquet garni, shiitake stems, and salt. Let the stock simmer gently for about 45 minutes.
· Pass the stock through a strainer or cheesecloth and let cool. Refrigerate for up to 3 days, or freeze.

- In a large bowl, combine the sherry, soy sauce, hoisin sauce, plum sauce, ginger, red pepper flakes, and honey. Place the duck in the bowl. If the marinade does not cover the duck completely, add water. Place in the refrigerator and let the duck marinate for 24 hours.
- When ready to roast the duck, preheat the oven to 350°F. Remove the duck from the marinade and reserve the marinade. Place the duck on a rack in a roasting pan and roast for about 1½ hours, basting every 10 minutes with the marinade, until the duck is done and the skin is crisp.

- Place the semolina, all-purpose flour, salt, and oil in a mixer fitted with a dough hook. Add the eggs and mix until the dough starts to form a ball.
- Remove from the mixer, cover with a towel, and let rest for a couple of hours in the refrigerator.
- Using a hand pasta machine, roll the dough to the thickness of the first setting and reserve in the refrigerator until ready to use.

Chinese-style roasted ducks are available from many Asian markets. If you want to roast your own, order a duck from an Asian butcher and ask them to air-dry it for you. It's a process that requires a little practice.

ROASTED CHINESE-STYLE DUCK

. . . .

2 cups dry sherry
1 cup light soy sauce
2 cups hoisin sauce
1 cup plum sauce
½ cup sliced fresh ginger
1 teaspoon red pepper flakes
½ cup honey
1 3½- to 4-pound roasting duck

Makes 1 duck

. . . .

Use this Egg Noodle Dough to make pasta sheets for cannelloni, or just to make fresh pasta.

EGG NOODLE DOUGH

. . . .

1½ cups fine semolina flour
1½ cups all-purpose flour
1 teaspoon salt
2 tablespoons olive oil
5 eggs

Makes 8 4×6-inch sheets

. . . .

GREEN CURRY PASTE

1 teaspoon minced garlic
2 medium shallots, minced
1 fresh coriander root or
    6 stems, chopped
1 stalk lemongrass, chopped
15 small green chilies, chopped
1 tablespoon kaffir lime zest
½ teaspoon green peppercorns
½ teaspoon roasted
    coriander seeds
¼ teaspoon cumin seeds
1 tablespoon shrimp paste
⅓ cup + 2 tablespoons coconut
    or vegetable oil

Makes about 1¼ cups

· Place the garlic, shallots, coriander root, lemongrass, and chilies in a mortar or food processor and lightly pound or process. Add the lime zest, peppercorns, coriander seeds, cumin seeds, and shrimp paste and pound until almost smooth. Lastly, add the coconut oil.

RED CURRY PASTE

15 dried red chilies
¼ cup chopped ginger
1 garlic clove, minced
1 fresh coriander root or
    6 stems, chopped
2 stalks lemongrass, chopped
¼ teaspoon pink peppercorns
½ teaspoon roasted
    coriander seeds
½ teaspoon roasted cumin seeds
½ teaspoon turmeric
Pinch of salt
1 teaspoon shrimp paste
⅓ cup vegetable oil

Makes about 1¼ cups

· Soften the chilies by soaking them in warm water for about 15 minutes. Chop the chilies and place them in a mortar or food processor with the ginger, garlic, coriander root, and lemongrass. Pound or process lightly, and add the peppercorns, coriander seeds, cumin seeds, turmeric, salt, and shrimp paste. Pound until smooth. Add the vegetable oil and mix thoroughly.

Appendix

Conversions

Liquid Measures

Fluid Ounces	*U.S. Measures*	*Imperial Measures*	*Milliliters*
	1 TSP	1 TSP	5
1/4	2 TSP	1 DESSERT SPOON	7
1/2	1 TBS	1 TBS	15
1	2 TBS	2 TBS	28
2	1/4 CUP	4 TBS	56
4	1/2 CUP OR 1/4 PINT		110
5		1/4 PINT OR 1 GILL	140
6	3/4 CUP		170
8	1 CUP OR 1/2 PINT		225
9			250, 1/4 LITER
10	1 1/4 CUPS	1/2 PINT	280
12	1 1/2 CUPS OR 3/4 PINT		240
15		3/4 PINT	420
16	2 CUPS OR 1 PINT		450
18	2 1/4 CUPS		500, 1/2 LITER
20	2 1/2 CUPS	1 PINT	560
24	3 CUPS OR 1 1/2 PINTS		675
25		1 1/4 PINTS	700
27	3 1/2 CUPS		750
30	3 3/4 CUPS	1 1/2 PINTS	840
32	4 CUPS OR 2 PINTS OR 1 QUART		900
35		1 1/4 PINTS	980
36	4 1/2 CUPS		1000, 1 LITER

Solid Measures

U.S. and Imperial Measures		*Metric Measures*	
Ounces	*Pounds*	*Grams*	*Kilos*
1		28	
2		56	
3 1/2		100	
4	1/4	112	
5		140	
6		168	
8	1/2	225	
9		250	1/4
12	3/4	340	
16	1	450	
18		500	1/2
20	1 1/4	560	
24	1 1/2	675	
27		750	3/4
28	1 3/4	780	
32	2	900	
36	2 1/4	1000	1
40	2 1/2	1100	
48	3	1350	
54		1500	1 1/2

Oven Temperature Equivalents

Fahrenheit	*Gas Mark*	*Celsius*	*Heat of Oven*
225	1/4	107	VERY COOL
250	1/2	121	VERY COOL
275	1	135	COOL
300	2	148	COOL
325	3	163	MODERATE
350	4	177	MODERATE
375	5	190	FAIRLY HOT
400	6	204	FAIRLY HOT
425	7	218	HOT
450	8	232	VERY HOT
475	9	246	VERY HOT

Photographic Prop Credits

Bamboo steamer courtesy of the Kauai Museum, Lihue, Kauai, Hawaii: page 6.

Bowls and plates by An American Craftsman, 317 Bleecker Street, New York, New York: pages 16, 26, 54, 177.

Ikat fabric, uli uli, coconut canteen, wood plate, and bowls by Stones at Kilohana, 3-2087 Kaumualii Highway, Lihue, Kauai, Hawaii: pages 54, 86.

Plates by Contemporary Porcelain Gallery, 105 Sullivan Street, New York, New York: pages 105, 166, 184.

Plate by Kong Lung Co., Lighthouse Road, Kilauea, Kauai, Hawaii: page 171.

Hawaiian Ingredients and Substitutions

Annato The hard, reddish seed of the annato tree, ground into powder or paste. Also called *achiote*.

Ahi The Hawaiian word for both yellowfin and bigeye tuna. If it is not available, substitute any fresh tuna.

Aku Skipjack tuna, which accounts for more than 50 percent of the annual catch by Hawaiian commercial fishermen. If it is not available, substitute any fresh tuna.

Ama ebi Sweet shrimp, recognizable by their long antennae. Substitute fresh or frozen shrimp.

Black sea bass Called *hapu'upu'u* in the Islands, the Hawaiian black sea bass is a kind of grouper. Substitute grouper.

Cellophane noodles Also called *bean threads,* made from the starch of green mung beans. Available in Asian markets.

Coconut milk A creamy liquid extracted from the grated flesh of fresh coconut. (The liquid found in a coconut is called *coconut water.*) Coconut milk is sold in Asian markets in cans or in the freezer section. Do not substitute sweetened coconut milk.

Chinese black mushrooms Flavorful dried mushrooms available in Asian markets. Soak in warm water before using.

Daikon A long, white Asian radish, served raw and cooked. Available at Asian markets.

Fish sauce A thin, brown, salty liquid made from salted fresh shrimp or fish, and an indispensable ingredient in Vietnamese, Thai, and Philippine cooking. It is used to flavor soups and sauces and is available in bottles at Asian markets. Don't be put off by its strong aroma.

Five-spice powder Made of equal parts of ground star anise, cinnamon, cloves, fennel seeds, and Szechuan pepper and used extensively in Chinese cooking. It goes well with all meats, and is available in Asian markets.

Garlic chives Also known as Chinese chives, these long, flat, green chives taste of both garlic and onion. Available fresh and frozen at Asian markets.

Green papaya Unripe papayas. Unlike ripe papayas, they are starchy in consistency.

Hawaiian sea salt Sea salt with a distinctive pink color, harvested on Kauai. Regular sea salt or kosher salt can be substituted.

Hoisin sauce A thick, soy-based sauce made from soybean flour, red beans, chili pepper, sugar, salt, garlic, and other spices, with a sweet, pungent taste. It is available in Asian markets.

Japanese eggplants Thin, purple eggplants that are not bitter and do not need to be salted before using. Available at Asian markets.

Jicama A large, bulbous root that resembles a brown turnip. Used raw and cooked. Available in Hispanic markets.

Kaffir lime leaves Kaffir limes are a citrus fruit grown in southeast Asia. The leaves of this tree are used in cooking. They are available fresh and dried, and impart their distinctive flavor to soups, sauces, and curries.

Kajiki The Hawaiian name for the Pacific blue marlin, a mild-flavored fish that usually weighs from 80 to 100 pounds. If you can't find it, substitute halibut or swordfish.

Kamaboko A firm, slightly rubbery-textured processed fish cake that is very popular in Japan. It is available in the refrigerated section of Asian markets.

Kamado A Japanese egg-shaped smoker that distributes smoke and heat very evenly.

Kamanu Also known as the rainbow runner or Hawaiian salmon, it has a mild flavor and is good for smoking. If you can't find it, substitute salmon.

Kiawe The Hawaiian name for mesquite. It is a short, strong tree that grows on the dry part of Kauai. The wood is aromatic and imparts a great flavor when used with charcoal.

Kim chee A pungent, fermented pickle made from chopped napa cabbage seasoned with salt, chili pepper, and garlic, available in Korean markets.

Koi tomatoes The most common tomatoes in Hawaii, grown in greenhouses. Substitute any ripe tomato.

Kumu A light red reef fish, also known as goatfish. Substitute red snapper.

Lemongrass A fragrant grass that grows profusely in the tropics, used extensively in Thai cooking. Use white, creamy part near the base of the stalk. Lemongrass is available at Asian markets.

Lilikoi The Hawaiian word for passion fruit, available at specialty markets. Passion fruit juice is also available.

Lotus root The root of a water lily, which resembles sausage links, available at Asian markets.

Luau leaves The leaves of the taro plant, used in laulau. Substitute spinach.

Lychee A sweet, round fruit covered with a spiny red skin. The flesh is white, with black seeds. Available fresh and canned in Asian markets.

Mahi-mahi Also known as dolphinfish. Widely available.

Manoa lettuce A leafy green lettuce. Substitute any leafy green lettuce.

Maui onions Delicate, sweet onions grown on Maui. Substitute sweet onions such as Vidalia onions.

Mirin Sweet, syrupy rice wine from Japan, used to flavor marinades and glazes. Available in Asian markets.

Mochiko flour A Japanese flour made from cooked glutenous rice, available at Asian markets.

Monchong Also known as the bigscale pomfret. Substitute halibut.

Mountain apple A member of the myrtle family, also